SCORPIO
2002

For Beth and Phil, with much love.
Have a very happy life together!

Most authors can only dream of being part of a successful publishing team producing a series of best-selling books, so I consider myself extremely lucky to be working with everyone at Constable & Robinson for a fifth year. Five years! It seems like only yesterday . . . As ever, it's been a pleasure to produce these books in tandem with Nicola Chalton, Nova Jayne Heath and Nick Robinson. Many thanks as well to Elaine Henderson for managing the project and special thanks to Jane Horwood for all her eagle-eyed editing skills, to Annie Lionnet for her wonderful back-up, to Bill Martin for his superstar qualities and to Chelsey Fox for being a super agent. What a team!

SCORPIO
2002

Jane Struthers

This is a Parragon Book
First published in 2001

Parragon
Queen Street House
4 Queen Street
Bath BA1 1HE
UK

Produced by Magpie Books, an imprint of
Constable & Robinson Ltd, London

Illustrations courtesy of Slatter-Anderson, London

ISBN 0-75255-708-4

A copy of the British Library Cataloguing-in-Publication Data is available from the British Library

Printed and bound in the EC

CONTENTS

Sun Sign Dates for 2002

Scorpio 24 October – 22 November

Sagittarius 23 November – 21 December

Capricorn 22 December – 20 January

Aquarius 21 January – 18 February

Pisces 19 February – 20 March

Aries 21 March – 20 April

Taurus 21 April – 21 May

Gemini 22 May – 21 June

Cancer 22 June – 22 July

Leo 23 July – 23 August

Virgo 24 August – 23 September

Libra 24 September – 23 October

INTRODUCTION

Dear Scorpio

Are you ready for a fabulous 2002? With the help of my astrological guide to the year, you'll be able to make the most of the benefits coming your way and steer around any possible pitfalls.

So what have I got lined up for you in this year's book? **Scorpio 2002** kicks off with a summary of what the year will bring for you in your relationships, health, money and career. After that comes your day by day guide to 2002, complete with at-a-glance charts for each month so you can get an idea of what's in store for you.

Your Scorpio Sun Sign tells you all sorts of fascinating information about yourself, including the way you handle your relationships, money, health and career. After that comes **Love and the Stars**, telling you how each sign gets along with all the other signs in the zodiac. You can start by reading all about your relationships and then you can discover how the other signs get on with you. If you want an instant assessment of how a relationship will work out, I've included two handy charts for you, so you can instantly see how you fare with other signs for love and sex, and also for friendship.

In **Your Potential and Creativity**, you can read about ways to express your sign's unique potential. These could introduce you to a new hobby and they might even lead you into a new career.

If you were born at the beginning or end of Scorpio and you aren't sure which sign you belong to, you'll love reading **Born on the Cusp?** because it will clear up the mystery at long last!

Have fun reading this book, and have a wonderful 2002!

Jane Struthers

THE YEAR 2002

Friends and Lovers

It's going to be a very busy year for your relationships. In fact, they are one of the highlights of 2002 and some of your partnerships won't be the same by the time 2003 rolls around. Before you start to panic, there may not be anything negative in this. For instance, one relationship may have gone from strength to strength, or you might be feeling relieved that a partnership is now over so you don't have to worry about it any longer.

This year is a good opportunity to take a close look at your most intimate relationships. Are you happy with them or is there room for improvement? If you suspect that your alliance with a certain person is coming to an end because you don't have anything in common any longer, the cracks between you will soon become apparent. You'll be able to decide whether to patch things up or say goodbye. In fact, any relationship that isn't working well will now start to show the strain. Rather than cling on to a partnership that is over in all but name, be prepared to admit that it's run its course and it's time to separate. It will help if you can acknowledge that this is just one of those things, rather than heaping blame on yourself – or on the other person.

If your Scorpio nature gives you a tendency to be jealous or possessive, you'll continue to battle with this in 2002. Do your best to overcome any urge to control your loved ones or to begrudge them other relationships, because that will only cause bad feeling between you.

The Eclipsed Full Moon in late November will give you the chance to sort out any long-running partnership problems. It will also show you where your loyalties – and those of your partners – lie.

Health

If you've started the year feeling rather flat and lethargic, how about arranging a holiday? It will do you good to have something to look forward to, even if you can only afford a very modest trip. It's not the cost that's important, it's the chance to spread your wings and have a change of scene that matters in 2002. If a holiday is out of the question, try to arrange some short breaks instead. They'll still have the desired effect of brightening your outlook and helping you to feel more optimistic.

Relationship problems may be getting you down at the moment, in which case they'll make you feel listless and depressed at times. Once again, it's important for you to counter this with activities that lift your spirits. Otherwise it will be horribly easy for worries to prey on your mind, and for you to frighten yourself by fantasizing about the worst things that can possibly happen.

From early August onwards, your work will keep you pretty busy. Try to balance this with plenty of relaxation, and also make sure you don't skimp too much on sleep and decent food. As a Scorpio you have incredible stamina and emotional energy, but even you need refuelling every now and then!

Money

Your attitude to money is very conservative this year. Even if you've got lots of cash rolling in, you will still feel as though hard times are just around the corner and will behave accordingly. That's because it's a year in which you prefer to save money rather than spend it. Whenever any extra money comes in, your natural instinct will be to keep a firm grip on it. Of course there will be occasions when you get the urge to splurge, but these won't happen very often. Most of the time you'll be looking at your bank account and wondering why there isn't more money in it, even if everyone else thinks it's bulging at the seams. You may also have to bail out a partner when they go through a lean patch, so that might be another reason to save your money.

If you've been playing hide and seek with the taxman in recent years, this may be the year in which you're caught! It will be far better to sort out your finances and get everything out into the open rather than prolong the agony of waiting to be nabbed.

Even though you won't have a lot of cash to spare in 2002, you'll want to make the best use of what you do have. Investigate sensible savings schemes, endowments, pensions and any other arrangements that will put your money to good use. Even if you sometimes invest on the stock exchange, you may be reluctant to take that sort of risk this year.

Career

If your career is connected with travel, higher education, religion, the law, philosophy or the environment, you can look forward to some bumper periods in 2002. Between the start of January and the beginning of August will be a great time to take your career to a higher level, and also to thoroughly enjoy what you do. New opportunities may open up, especially if they offer you the chance to broaden your experiences and branch out in different directions. You'll also enjoy rising to challenges that stretch your mental abilities and give you something interesting to get your teeth into.

You'll be in great demand from early August onwards. This might be when you finally hit the big time. You could get a better job or be offered some good promotion chances in your current job. You will also discover, much to your delight, that you're in the right place at the right time. This will seem to happen without any input from you, and you may well have good reason to thank your lucky stars.

If you want to take some risks and go out on a limb, 2002 is the year to give it a go. You might be a lot more successful than you could ever have imagined!

Your Day by Day Guide

JANUARY AT A GLANCE

Love	♥ ♥ ♥
Money	£ $
Career	💻 💻 💻
Health	☼ ☼ ☼

• *Tuesday 1 January* •

It's a brilliant start to 2002 because you're fired with enthusiasm and optimism about what the coming year will bring. Even if 2001 failed to live up to your expectations, you have high hopes that 2002 will be a lot more productive. How about starting that process by thinking about what you want to achieve over the next twelve months? Anything that broadens your mental and physical horizons will be a really good bet.

• *Wednesday 2 January* •

If you're back at work today you'll be happy to get right down to things. You don't want to waste time and your industrious attitude may make a big impression on a VIP or boss. This is certainly a good opportunity to put across your ideas, and you'll be a big hit if you're attending a meeting or interview. There may also be good news about some money connected with your job.

• *Thursday 3 January* •

Your thoughts take a rather nostalgic turn today, and during the next few weeks there will be phases when you really enjoy reflecting on the past. You might even be inspired to dig out old keepsakes and mementoes to have another look at them. If one of your New Year resolutions is to sort out your photos and get them into some sort of order, you'll enjoy starting that project now.

• *Friday 4 January* •

It won't take much to get a certain someone all fired up today. The trouble is, they may get so carried away that they end up going over the top. For instance, you might arouse their anger and end up being on the receiving end of a furious outburst. On the other hand, maybe you're the one who's got steam coming out of both ears and who's looking for an outlet? Don't make anyone your scapegoat.

• *Saturday 5 January* •

You're full of confidence about what the future will bring today, so it's great for making plans about what to do this January and beyond. Any hint of an adventure or challenge is right up your street now because you certainly don't want to play safe or hedge your bets. As a result, you may take on more than you can comfortably handle, or agree to something that will trigger second thoughts later on.

• *Sunday 6 January* •

There's a lot of tension in the air today. Perhaps it's simply because you're feeling flat after all the recent festivities? Or maybe you're worried about something and it's starting to get on your nerves? Whatever's wrong, try to get it out in the open now. If you're annoyed about someone's behaviour, it will be far better all round to say so than to allow it to fester inside you and erupt later on in a tirade of pent-up frustration.

• *Monday 7 January* •

Anything or anyone that allows you to escape harsh reality is fine by you today! You simply aren't interested. This could cause problems if you're expected to deal with hard facts or complicated details because it will be a struggle to keep your mind on what you're doing. You'll be far more comfortable when allowing your imagination to take flight or when doing something creative.

• *Tuesday 8 January* •

You feel wonderfully sociable and friendly today, and you won't want to spend too much time by yourself if you can possibly help it. Even chatting to someone over a cup of coffee will be good fun, or you might decide to phone a chum to catch up on all the recent news. This is also a good day to get involved in a local enterprise or neighbourhood scheme. Not only will you feel you're doing your bit, you'll also enjoy the social aspect of the project.

• *Wednesday 9 January* •

There's such a strong mental link between you and a loved one today that there's almost no need for words. You might discover remarkable ESP between you or you may be in complete accord about something so you speak with one mind. It feels good to know that you share this rapport and you'll be able to draw on it in the future. You may also enjoy reminiscing about the past.

• *Thursday 10 January* •

Put your mind to work today because you're in a very practical and sensible mood. It's an especially good day to think about your official and joint finances, especially if you want to organize them better or you're considering making some constructive changes. If you've been contemplating a house move but don't know how much money you've got to play with, contact an expert now so you can see exactly where you stand.

• *Friday 11 January* •

Someone's high spirits are good fun at first but they may start to wear you down after a while. This person may seem a bit like Tigger – very bouncy and extremely tiring! Be careful when dealing with financial matters because it won't take much to aggravate you. This is especially likely if you're out on the town with someone – there could be a dispute about your share of the bill or they may ask you for something you can't give them. Proceed with caution.

• *Saturday 12 January* •

Yesterday's bad mood has evaporated, leaving you in a very magnanimous mood. You're prepared to give the other person the benefit of the doubt, or to apologize if necessary. You have far more important things to do now than to waste time on petty grievances. One thing on your agenda might be arranging a forthcoming journey or holiday. If you've got itchy feet right now you'll be longing to get away.

• *Sunday 13 January* •

Today's New Moon signals the start of a new phase in the way you communicate with others. For instance, you may feel it's high time you bought a new television or computer. Or you might want to sort out the recent difficulties you've been having with a certain person. If you're aware that your relationships often seem to fall into a particular pattern that isn't very helpful, start thinking about how you can change things to make them easier.

• *Monday 14 January* •

The shops are calling! If you've been strong-willed enough to resist the lure of the January sales so far, your powers of resistance are now starting to crumble. Besides, you may have spotted something in a shop window that you've just got to have. It's a super day for buying a new outfit or accessory. It's also a good chance to kiss and make up with someone, especially if you want to put yesterday's resolutions into action with as little delay as possible.

• *Tuesday 15 January* •

Keep in touch with members of the family today. You'll thoroughly enjoy talking to them. Ideally, you should gather lots of your nearest and dearest around you, but if that isn't possible at least talk to some of them on the phone or write some letters. A chat with someone you know inside out could be very productive, especially if one of you has something to get off your chest.

• *Wednesday 16 January* •

Familiarity breeds restlessness today. You'll soon start to feel stagnant and stale if you're cooped up in one place for too long, and you'll also feel like screaming with frustration if you can't break away from your usual Wednesday routine. However, matters may be taken out of your hands by unexpected events or a surprise visitor. Yet, strangely enough, you may resent any interruptions even though part of you longs for them. It's an odd day.

• *Thursday 17 January* •

You're feeling great! You're in a terrific mood and are determined to get the most out of the day even if it doesn't seem very promising. It's your positive attitude and your cheerful mood that will make all the difference. If you've been toying with the idea of getting to know someone better, this is a great opportunity to chat to them and see if you hit it off.

• *Friday 18 January* •

Better roll up your sleeves because a lot of hard work is coming your way over the next few weeks. Not that you'll mind because you'll like the feeling that you're doing whatever you can to help, whether it's through your job or some other aspect of your life. What you won't appreciate, however, is any hint that you're being taken for granted or even being played for a fool. But don't confront anyone about this until you're sure of the facts. Things may not be entirely what they seem.

• *Saturday 19 January* •

Between now and mid-February is a marvellous chance to enjoy your home comforts as much as possible. Your idea of heaven now may be to curl up at home at every opportunity and revel in having your nearest and dearest around you. If you're feeling rather more energetic than that, how about giving your home a new look for the new year? Maybe you could give your interior design skills a whirl?

• *Sunday 20 January* •

With your thoughts turning to home and family, you certainly won't enjoy being in unfamiliar surroundings over the next four weeks. In fact, there will be times when you feel distinctly uncomfortable when away from your own four walls. This will be a marvellous chance to connect with your roots in some way. That might mean being with relatives or it could involve tracing back your ancestry and incorporating some of it in your everyday life.

• *Monday 21 January* •

You need to tiptoe around on eggshells today if you're going to keep a certain someone sweet. They're liable to go off pop at the first thing that annoys them, and your initial reaction is to avoid this by pacifying them as much as possible. But where will this leave you, apart from exhausted and tense? Maybe it would be a better tactic to allow the inevitable row to come to a head, so you can get it out of the way. Besides, it seems you both need to clear the air.

• *Tuesday 22 January* •

Unfortunately the atmosphere still leaves a lot to be desired. You may still be having problems with the person who was so difficult yesterday, or perhaps you've caught their mood and now you're the one who's stamping around under a thunder cloud? Whatever is wrong, get it out into the open. However, try not to get sucked into listing your grievances about every little thing from A to Z – it will reduce the power of your argument. Stick to the essentials.

• *Wednesday 23 January* •

Concentrate on your home and joint finances today. You could come up with some great ideas for improving things, not only immediately but in the longer term. You may also gain important insights into better ways to deal with certain people in your life, especially if your relationship with them is challenging but necessary. Trust in the intuitions that come to you now and be prepared to act on them.

• *Thursday 24 January* •

You feel relaxed and happy today, and you want to spread a little sunshine without being cloying or too sugary-sweet. All you need do is be yourself! It's an especially good day for being with loved ones. If you're determined to act on yesterday's decision to improve your rapport with a certain person, now is the perfect time to begin. Start by seeing things from their point of view – it isn't as difficult as you might think.

• *Friday 25 January* •

You're in a wonderfully dreamy mood today and you don't want to come down to earth for longer than necessary. You're having too much fun wrapped up in your own little world. This is fantastic if you're spending the day with a special person or you've already promised yourself to turn today into a mini retreat from the rest of the world. However, it may be difficult to function if you're expected to do anything very detailed or fiddly. Can't you postpone it for a few days?

• *Saturday 26 January* •

You're going through a very important phase in your relationships at the moment because you're feeling very understanding of other people. Rather than feel annoyed with them for not being more like you, you're completely happy to allow them to be themselves, whatever and whoever that might be. This is another day when your acceptance of other people's quirks and foibles helps you to appreciate them better.

• *Sunday 27 January* •

Someone has a lot to say today! They're chatting away non-stop. Although you'll enjoy this at first, after a while you may begin to wish you could get a word in edgeways! Or maybe it's the other way round and you're the one who's barely drawn breath all day? Whichever it is, you'll certainly enjoy talking and hearing about family matters and episodes from the past.

• *Monday 28 January* •

If you've been trying to juggle the demands of your home life with the responsibilities of your career recently, the coming two weeks will reveal how well you're doing. Today's Full Moon will highlight any problems you're experiencing in balancing these two areas of your life, forcing you to do something about them. The answer may be a lot simpler than you think, such as asking someone to help out or doing some delegating.

• *Tuesday 29 January* •

Right on cue, you encounter some of the difficulties that were mentioned yesterday. You may have to reassure someone who feels they're being neglected or coming a poor second to other areas of your life. There's also a chance that a woman is jealous of your seeming ability to cope so well with all the demands that you currently face. Even if you beg to disagree with her, she won't believe you.

• *Wednesday 30 January* •

Pay attention to your health today. If you're feeling great at the moment you'll want to stay that way, so think about how you can do that. And if you're feeling slightly under the weather at the moment, consider how you can improve your well-being. A complementary therapy or treatment may appeal. You might also realize that changing certain things at home will make a big difference, for instance buying more comfortable pillows so you get a better night's sleep.

• *Thursday 31 January* •

This is a marvellous chance to scrutinize your finances, especially if you need to bring them up to date or you want to get to the bottom of a current mystery. You won't rest until you've sorted everything out. All the same, try not to get so caught up in tiny details that you pursue them to the point of compulsion. If you are the sort of Scorpio who can get bogged down in nit-picking details, today may help you to understand that this can be counterproductive.

FEBRUARY AT A GLANCE

Love	♥ ♥ ♥ ♥ ♥
Money	£ $
Career	💻 💻 💻
Health	☼ ☼ ☼ ☼

• *Friday 1 February* •

You enjoy plenty of harmony with a certain person today. It does you good to know that you're able to establish such a strong rapport at the moment. Even if relations aren't always easy between you, you are currently able to make up for that. You may even feel quite overwhelmed when you realize how much this person means to you. On a more mundane note, this is a good day to buy items that will improve your home in some way.

• *Saturday 2 February* •

The harmonious atmosphere continues today and long may it last! It's a super day for surrounding yourself with some of your nearest and dearest, and it's perfect if you're planning a family get-together. Listen carefully if someone wants to confide in you, because they're doing you an honour by talking to you in such depth. If you're the one who needs a sympathetic ear, you'll soon find the ideal person.

• *Sunday 3 February* •

You're in the mood for some adventure today, especially if it takes you out of your usual Sunday routine or offers you a chance to explore the world in some way. Planning your next long journey or holiday is right up your street now, so watch a holiday programme on TV, or leaf through some brochures and see if anywhere appeals. You'll also enjoy talking to someone who comes from another country or culture.

• *Monday 4 February* •

Communications need special care from today because they could easily start to unravel and leave your nerves feeling frayed over the next four days. During this time you'd be wise to avoid signing important contracts or putting anything else in writing, in case you make a mistake or aren't yet in possession of all the facts. Short journeys may also be prone to disruption so you'll have to be patient.

• *Tuesday 5 February* •

It's very difficult to get on with your usual Tuesday schedule because there are some irritating interruptions to contend with. There could be last-minute changes of plan connected with your home or a member of the family. For instance, if you're waiting at home to receive a delivery or because an appliance needs to be repaired, there could be delays or even a no-show. You have been warned!

• *Wednesday 6 February* •

Take a good look around your home today. Do you like what you see or are you reminded yet again of that pile of clutter waiting to be sorted out or some other blot on the landscape that you've been promising yourself you'll tackle one of these days? If so, this is a great chance to set the ball rolling. You'll really enjoy doing some tidying up, especially if that means throwing away items that you no longer need or which are only gathering dust.

• *Thursday 7 February* •

Your home life brings you some surprises today. There might be an unexpected visitor or you could find a possession that you thought had been lost forever. Take care when handling a relative who wants to strike out on their own in some way.

They need to express their independence, even if they don't follow it through. They won't like it if you try to clip their wings or hold them back.

• *Friday 8 February* •

Thank goodness communications start to return to normal today. With luck, you won't have suffered much disruption so you won't have to spend long making up for lost time. If you need to reach a decision about a neighbour or close relative, or about a child's education, this is a very good opportunity to finally make up your mind. You're in an extremely incisive mood today.

• *Saturday 9 February* •

Keep calm! Unfortunately that's easier said than done because it won't take much to get you jumping up and down with irritation. What's wrong? Your patience may be tested to the limit by someone who wants to take their time over things while you would prefer that they jumped to it right this second. Be very careful if you're driving today because hasty actions could lead to minor prangs. And don't be tempted to do any speeding!

• *Sunday 10 February* •

You have a real way with words today. It means you're very communicative and chatty. You may even have so much to say that no one else can get a word in edgeways! It's a super day for putting across your point of view but do try to pause for breath every now and then so it can be a proper conversation rather than a lecture! You may also get a lot more phone calls and e-mails than usual. It's a busy day!

• *Monday 11 February* •

You're determined to put everything you've got into your work today. If this is the start of your working week, there's no danger of you being beset by the Monday morning blues. Quite the reverse! You may get through a lot more work than usual, while colleagues can only watch in amazement. It's also a good day to clear up any problems connected with your salary or some work perks.

• *Tuesday 12 February* •

Whatever else you have planned for the rest of February, try to make enjoyment one of your top priorities. You probably won't need much persuading! This will be a marvellous chance to celebrate life in all its glory, from going to parties to expressing your creativity. There may also be lots of happiness courtesy of your love life, with a certain someone making it plain that they can't live without you. Perfect timing for Valentine's Day!

• *Wednesday 13 February* •

You're very interested in improving your domestic life at the moment and you could come up with some very clever ideas today. However, some of them may seem rather radical or unconventional, which could cause a few ruffled feathers among any sticklers for tradition in your family circle. But you're currently interested in moving forwards and making progress, not in clinging to the status quo, and you aren't impressed by their arguments.

• *Thursday 14 February* •

If you're looking forward to a memorable Valentine's Day you won't be disappointed. Powerful currents of emotion are flowing between you and you-know-who, creating a hothouse atmosphere of heightened reactions and sexual tension. Everything will be fine provided you're both happy with this intensity of feeling. But there will be ructions if one of you starts to feel swamped or suffocated and needs to retreat.

• *Friday 15 February* •

You're brimming with optimism today but try not to let it get out of hand. You'll tread a fine line between positive thinking and unrealistic ideas. Be especially careful if you're at work because you could easily take on more responsibility than you can comfortably handle. This will lead to embarrassment later on when you have to admit that you've bitten off more than you can chew. It will be even worse if you have to let someone down.

• *Saturday 16 February* •

Today is one of the highlights of February, so give it all you've got! It's fantastic for putting all the chores to one side and concentrating on fun, fun, fun. If you're going to a party, wedding or some other social gathering, then you'll be the life and soul of the entire proceedings. And if Valentine's Day failed to live up to expectations, celebrate it again today!

• *Sunday 17 February* •

If you really pushed the boat out yesterday you'll probably want to take things nice and easy today. So it's very fortunate that you're all set for a relaxing day. You'll thoroughly enjoy pottering about at home. If you're feeling a little more energetic, how about doing some entertaining? It's great for inviting a colleague over to your place so you can get to know them better. Or maybe you fancy a family gathering?

• *Monday 18 February* •

Life is starting to take on a very light-hearted tone, and over the next four weeks you'll want to place the accent on enjoyment and pleasure whenever you get the chance. It's also a super time to be with some of your favourite people because you'll really appreciate their company. If you're single at the moment and you wish you weren't, keep an eye open for Mr or Ms Right who might be coming along any minute now!

• *Tuesday 19 February* •

Good luck when handling a certain person today. You'll need it! They're determined to argue the toss at every opportunity. If you say something's white, they'll tell you it's black. They may even show every sign of going out of their way to be irritating, unreliable and a complete pain in the neck. What can you do about this? Not much, it seems, except grit your teeth and give them a piece of your mind when it all gets beyond a joke. At least it won't last long.

• *Wednesday 20 February* •

There's a lot of tension in the air today, leading to a fraught atmosphere and a sense of gathering storms. If you can't bear tiptoeing around trying to be on your best behaviour, it will be better to challenge the person who's creating this feeling and find out what's wrong. But don't be surprised if you're told that you have somehow been adding to the problem through your attitude. Before you explode with anger, think about it. This person may have a point.

• *Thursday 21 February* •

Turn your attention to your joint and official finances today. You need to tie up any loose ends before they trip you up or cause embarrassment. This is also an excellent day to provide for your future financial security in some way. Talk to an expert about starting a pension plan, taking out a long-term investment, or anything else that makes good use of your money.

• *Friday 22 February* •

Make the most of today's fabulous atmosphere. You're eager to get on well with everyone you meet, even if that means letting them call the shots or turning a blind eye to previous problems between you. Quite frankly, you're in such a magnanimous mood right now that you aren't prepared to let past quarrels stand in the way of what looks like being a very happy day. People will admire you for it.

• *Saturday 23 February* •

You're in a very practical and matter-of-fact mood today, especially when it comes to your finances and your domestic arrangements. You're blessed with a lot of common sense right now, helping you to reach important decisions without rushing into them or taking panic measures. But do make sure you consult the people involved before taking decisions that could have a big effect on them.

• *Sunday 24 February* •

This is another day when you're ready to have fun at every opportunity. Speaking of which, some super opportunities could be in the pipeline. You'll certainly want to explore every avenue open to you at the moment, even if it offers quite a challenge or is something you're trying out for the first time. The only possible snag is a tendency to take on more than you can manage. Other than that, you're poised for success.

• *Monday 25 February* •

Keep calm! It's very tempting to get het up today, especially if you're trying to meet a tight deadline or you feel that everyone is on your back and you can't satisfy their demands. You may also get bogged down in reams of red tape, making you feel that you're getting nowhere fast. If you do have to deal with officialdom right now, you may encounter someone who's determined to follow the rule book to the point of being small-minded and intransigent.

• *Tuesday 26 February* •

Feelings run high today, especially in matters of the heart. There is tremendous intensity between you and a certain person. You may feel as though you're caught up in a romantic drama that wouldn't be out of place on the silver screen. It's full of highs and lows, and if you have a row you'll really enjoy kissing and making up later on! But be careful about mixing love and money because they'll be like oil and water and could easily lead to resentment and arguments.

• *Wednesday 27 February* •

Today's Full Moon signals that it's time to think again about your hopes and wishes for the future. Are they going according to plan or do you need to take remedial action? Mull things over during the coming fortnight and be prepared to scrap some projects and start again from scratch if need be. That will be far more productive in the long run than wasting time flogging a dead horse.

• *Thursday 28 February* •

You're really only interested in being with friends and loved ones today. Anything else is merely an inconvenience that you want to get out of the way as quickly as possible. If you're currently a member of a group or organization, you'll really enjoy getting involved in it right now. And if you're attending a meeting, you might encounter someone who will turn out to be a good contact.

MARCH AT A GLANCE

Love	♥ ♥ ♥ ♥ ♥
Money	£ $ £ $ £
Career	💻 💻 💻 💻 💻
Health	☼ ☼ ☼ ☼ ☼

• *Friday 1 March* •

Between now and the middle of April you'll feel the urge to channel stacks of energy into your one-to-one relationships. You'll make an extra effort to keep in touch with people and to get on well with them, and you'll be annoyed if they don't reciprocate. However, this could easily lead to problems because you may be quite vociferous about getting what you want. It will be tempting to forget about the need for give and take, but do so at your peril!

• *Saturday 2 March* •

You get an example of the dangers of forcing your ideas on others today when you're on the receiving end of someone who's being pushy and forceful. If only they would calm down a little, everything would be great! If you've been feeling annoyed with someone, all the tension between you may come to a head now, erupting in a volcanic outburst. It's good to get it all out in the open but don't go OTT!

• *Sunday 3 March* •

The atmosphere is starting to calm down and you're feeling much more relaxed as a result. This is a fantastic day for talking to loved ones about plans that concern all of you. For example, if you're considering doing some DIY at home, this is a great opportunity to discuss it with everyone and make sure they all agree with your plans. It's important to get everyone's agreement before going ahead. It will also be helpful to work out a budget.

• *Monday 4 March* •

You're in a very easy-going and happy mood today. Long may it last! Whatever you have planned for the day, you'll want to enjoy yourself as much as possible. You may even decide to postpone any chores or unpleasant duties until tomorrow, so you don't spoil the current mood. A certain person gives you good reason to celebrate because they're so smitten by you at the moment that you feel you're walking on air.

• *Tuesday 5 March* •

This is a good day to tackle your finances but be warned that you could easily start to take it all very seriously. If you're not very happy with the current state of your bank balance you may even press the panic button and allow worries to overwhelm you. However, before you start chewing your fingernails down to the quick, bear in mind that you're probably seeing things in a rather doom-laden and pessimistic light. The situation may not be nearly as bad as it seems.

• *Wednesday 6 March* •

You can't live someone else's life for them today, even though you may want to. As soon as you start telling someone what you think they should do, or worrying about the choices they've made, they'll make it very plain that they're annoyed with you. So you'll have to bite your lip if you think a loved one is going off the rails or heading for trouble. This is definitely not the day to give them a gentle warning or some words of advice. Try again tomorrow.

• *Thursday 7 March* •

You have no qualms about putting your thoughts into words today and you'll get your point across in no uncertain terms. No one could accuse you of beating about the bush! This is just what you need if you've been nerving yourself up to say your piece, and you'll also manage to stop yourself before you say too much. It's an especially good day to sort out problems with close relatives, neighbours and partners.

• *Friday 8 March* •

If you're still concerned about the current state of your finances, this is a good day to do something about it. Maybe you need to reduce your outgoings drastically? If so, you're in the mood to make some sweeping economies, particularly when it comes to cutting back on luxuries and what now seem like fripperies. Even though such cost-cutting might seem a tough prospect at other times, today you're quite confident that it's the only answer.

• *Saturday 9 March* •

The past few days have been tense and difficult, so how about burning off the negative effects with some physical exercise? You're feeling very energetic and lively, so you'll relish the thought of going for a brisk walk, jogging round the block, or visiting the gym. You may even want to take someone along for company, and also so you can outclass them – you're feeling very competitive right now!

• *Sunday 10 March* •

In complete contrast to yesterday's buzzy mood, you now want to flop and take things easy. Your idea of heaven is to take the phone off the hook and be deliciously lazy at home. You might potter about in the garden or do some cooking, but you don't want to exert yourself if you don't have to. It's good to be in the restful company of some of your nearest and dearest, but you may want to avoid anyone who's too demanding.

• *Monday 11 March* •

Over the next two weeks you'll thoroughly enjoy using your brain. It doesn't matter whether you do this for work or leisure – the pleasure will be the same. Quizzes, puzzles and competitions will all attract you, and you might even win a prize if you're lucky. You'll also enjoy being with children, but be warned that they'll be very lively and there could be some practical jokes.

• *Tuesday 12 March* •

You're very keen to enjoy yourself today but you'll have to get the chores out of the way first. Even though you're tempted to forget about your present duties, it would be a good idea to sort them out before you down tools for the day. If you're going to a social event today keep an eye out for someone who comes from another country or culture and who will be fascinating company.

• *Wednesday 13 March* •

A loved one does their best to throw their weight around today and it leaves a nasty taste in your mouth. They're very keen to impose their will on you, whether you like it or not. And, guess what, you *don't* like it! It might be tempting to give them a taste of their own medicine but this will only exacerbate the situation and bring you down to their level. Nevertheless, there's nothing to stop you saying what you think of their behaviour.

• *Thursday 14 March* •

There's plenty to look forward to during the coming fortnight, thanks to today's very favourable New Moon. The accent will be on your love life and on anything else that brings you pleasure. For instance, activities that bring out your true self and allow you to express your creative talents will be right up your street. There may also be excellent news about a child or forthcoming celebration.

• *Friday 15 March* •

Make the most of the ideas that come into your mind now, because some of them will be worth their weight in gold. What's more, you'll really enjoy this creative and inventive phase. This is also a marvellous day to give your brain an outing, especially if you get involved in a project that really makes you think or increases your experience of the world. This could be anything from arranging a long-distance journey to a country you've never visited before to teaching yourself about a fascinating subject.

• *Saturday 16 March* •

If this is your day of rest, you'll enjoy extracting every ounce of enjoyment out of it. Perhaps all you want is to laze away at home with your feet up, or maybe you're going to pamper yourself from top to toe. Being with loved ones will bring you a lot of happiness, even if you're only chatting to them over a cup of tea. You'll enjoy reminiscing about the past. If you're at work, there may be a romantic atmosphere between you and a colleague. Watch this space!

• *Sunday 17 March* •

You're in a very sober and practical mood today. It's fabulous for sorting out your priorities and tackling them in order of importance. The last thing you want to do now is waste time or get sidetracked by what you see as silly distractions. Sadly, loved ones may disagree with you about what's most important. For example, someone may need your attention over something that you consider to be a trifling matter but which is all-consuming to them at the moment. Make allowances for them!

• *Monday 18 March* •

You're in a very punchy, dynamic mood today. You won't suffer fools gladly either, as you'll make more than plain. It's fantastic for putting across your point of view or standing up for yourself because you're so full of confidence. But this attitude may cause wounded feelings among people who aren't in such a robust mood. Choose your words carefully when talking to someone who's very vulnerable right now.

• *Tuesday 19 March* •

What a fantastic day! You're in a very sunny temper and you're at pains to hit it off with everyone around you. If you suspect that you trod on someone's toes yesterday or hurt them in some way, you'll be quick to apologize. You may even buy them a little treat to reinforce your message. Your love life is blossoming today, and if you've been waiting to hear from you-know-who, you might soon be jumping for joy.

• *Wednesday 20 March* •

Once again you're in a very easy-going mood. You want to give everyone a fair hearing so you're eager to listen to what they have to say. It's great if you're taking part in a discussion because you're being so fair-minded and objective. It's also good for talking to partners and loved ones, especially if you've been trying to make them see a situation from your point of view. You may have more success today by taking things gently than on a day when you use more heavy-handed methods.

• *Thursday 21 March* •

Scrutinize your finances today, especially if it's been a while since you paid much attention to them. If you're puzzled by a mystery entry on your credit card statement or you have some questions for your bank, sort things out now while you're in the mood to get to the bottom of the problem. No one will be able to fob you off with lame excuses because you'll see straight through them.

• *Friday 22 March* •

If you still have things to sort out after yesterday, carry on the good work. You're on a roll at the moment! However, make sure you keep things in proportion because it won't take much for you to get a bee in your bonnet about certain situations. If that happens, you'll want to pursue them to the nth degree and that may lead to you going round in circles. Do your best to remain objective and rational right now.

• *Saturday 23 March* •

You have a very enquiring mind today and it will take you off on some wonderful journeys of exploration. You want to look further than the end of your nose and you're intrigued by ideas and theories that stretch your imagination or suggest there's more to life than meets the eye. You might be intrigued by spiritual, religious or philosophical subjects, especially if they raise more questions than they answer.

• *Sunday 24 March* •

If you're at work today you'll want to give it everything you've got. Being of service to others is important to you right now, and you're quite prepared to put your own needs second today if that will enable you to help someone who's in need. Even if you aren't at work you'll find ways to be of assistance to people. Perhaps an older friend or relative would like you to run some errands for them?

• *Monday 25 March* •

Someone is very forceful today. It may be the sheer force of their personality or they may be on a personal crusade that makes them appear formidable. Either way, you'll want to treat them with care in case they lose their temper with you. Alternatively, you'll be the one who's firing on all cylinders and being rather intimidating into the bargain. It's a good day for proving to someone that you mean business, but don't play the heavy if it isn't necessary because it could provoke an unpleasant response in the other person.

• *Tuesday 26 March* •

Hobbies and other leisure activities are right up your street today. You feel as though you need a short breather while you recharge your batteries. You'll also enjoy being with friends right now, especially if they feel more like kindred spirits. If you've been considering joining a club or society that caters for one of your interests but you're unsure whether it's right for you, see if you can find out more about it now.

• *Wednesday 27 March* •

You'll achieve a tremendous amount at work today. You're feeling very industrious but you're also boosted by a strong self-confidence and a solid conviction that you'll do everything well. This is great up to a point because it will help you to surmount any hurdles that would usually faze you. However, try not to let this attitude get out of hand and make you appear arrogant or too big for your boots.

• *Thursday 28 March* •

What's worrying you? Something is nagging away at the back of your mind and, whether you realize it or not, it's using up a lot of energy. Today's Full Moon is telling you that it's about time you took some constructive action. Either do something that will help you to sort out this problem or, if it's insoluble, alter your attitude towards it so it no longer dominates your life. You may not be able to do this overnight but at least take a step in the right direction.

• *Friday 29 March* •

From today, start thinking about your work and your daily routine. Are you happy with your life at the moment or do you long to make some changes? If your current job no longer has anything to offer you, it's time to look for something with better prospects. Scan the newspaper adverts, sign up with an employment agency or talk to someone who can steer you in the right direction. If you're bored with the shape of your days, see if you can inject more mental stimulus into them.

• *Saturday 30 March* •

If there's a big attraction going on at the moment between you and a colleague, you get another dose of it today. You might flirt outrageously with one another or exchange meaningful looks. Where's it all going to end? At this stage it's probably mostly a bit of fun but you should ask yourself whether you want to take it further. It's not fair to tease someone who is taking you seriously if you have no intention of following it through.

• *Sunday 31 March* •

It's been a busy month and all you want to do today is flop and relax whenever you get the chance. Being in restful surroundings will do you the world of good, whether you stay at home or head for one of your favourite beauty spots. Speaking of beauty, you may be tempted to pamper yourself with some luxurious creams or scented oils. You will also enjoy being with some of your nearest and dearest.

APRIL AT A GLANCE

Love	♥ ♥ ♥ ♥ ♥
Money	£ $ £ $
Career	💻 💻 💻 💻 💻
Health	☼ ☼ ☼ ☼ ☼

• *Monday 1 April* •

One-to-one relationships enter a wonderful new phase from today, becoming much easier and more harmonious than they've been lately. It's exactly what you need if you want to kiss and make up with someone, or simply try to get on a better footing with them. This shouldn't be too difficult over the next six weeks, especially if you're prepared to nibble away at some humble pie or admit that you've been in the wrong.

• *Tuesday 2 April* •

Get to grips with domestic finances today, especially if you're fed up with not knowing exactly where you stand. It's not the sort of position any Scorpio wants to be in! Go through bills and direct debits, just to make sure everything is ticking over nicely. This is also an excellent day to sort out your emotional priorities. Be prepared to look deep into your heart to examine your feelings about certain people in your life. It will be a very instructive process.

• *Wednesday 3 April* •

Pull out all the stops if you want to charm someone into submission today. You've got the happy knack of knowing exactly the right thing to say, which is very handy if you want to get back in someone's good books. Any sort of social event is a real pleasure now because you'll make a big effort to get on well with everyone and it will be more than repaid. You might also make a new contact in the process.

• *Thursday 4 April* •

Put your imagination to good use today. You could come up with some great ideas for ways of improving your home life, even if they strike you as very minor. That's not what's important right now. If you've been wondering how to help a loved one, you might come up with some good ideas. Even talking to them so they can pour out their heart to you will be a help.

• *Friday 5 April* •

Energy surges through you today, making you a real live wire. You're especially good at saying what you think and defending your ideas, so woe betide anyone who tries to get the better of you intellectually. You'll wipe the floor with them, without being cruel or unpleasant. There could be a slight sense of competition between you and a certain person. What's that all about?

• *Saturday 6 April* •

It's a day for downing tools and doing as little as possible! Ideally, you should be in familiar or beautiful surroundings (or both!), relaxing and taking life easy. If you're at home, try to postpone any strenuous chores until another day when you're more in the mood for them. Your thoughts may drift off into all sorts of directions but don't be surprised if waves of nostalgia wash over you, making you feel quite sentimental.

• *Sunday 7 April* •

In complete contrast to yesterday, you're feeling energetic and lively. You also crave other people's company and will soon get fed up on your own. Anything that seems like a party or celebration is right up your street now, so how about arranging an impromptu get-together if you don't have anything planned? If you're looking for love, you could find it today. You'll certainly find plenty of enjoyment.

• *Monday 8 April* •

Has someone got out of bed on the wrong side? It certainly seems that way, given their thunderous mood and their tendency to bite your head off as soon as look at you. It's obvious that they're spoiling for a fight but try not to make matters worse by unconsciously (or consciously!) goading them into it. If you're the one wearing the scowl, do your best to direct your anger at the real cause of the problem rather than being cross with everyone and everything.

• *Tuesday 9 April* •

Someone's in a very naïve and idealistic mood today. They have no desire to face up to the facts and prefer to put their head in the sand. If you're trying to deal with this person you'll soon become exasperated by what you view as their inability to see the truth. However, it's highly likely that you're also reluctant to see things and people in their true light. Postpone making any important decisions until you're in a more realistic mood.

• *Wednesday 10 April* •

Be very careful today because you've been gripped by the desire to assert your independence come what may. Although there's nothing wrong with wanting to go your own way, you may do it in a rather heavy-handed manner because you're so determined to get your point across. As a result, if anyone offers objections to what you're doing, you'll react as though your very survival is at stake. It may help to do something very strenuous so you can work off some of your nervous tension.

• *Thursday 11 April* •

If you're at work today you'll be very keen to do your fair share. You may even get carried away and do more than is strictly necessary! Although this may be commendable, try not to make a rod for your own back by agreeing to do things that you can't really manage. A colleague may be rather full of themselves now, and you'll wonder whether you dare take them down a peg or two.

• *Friday 12 April* •

You're in a very inventive and clever frame of mind today. You'll come up with some excellent insights into the current state of your life, and also into certain people's behaviour. If you've been trying to solve a problem connected with your home, family, health or work, mull it over again today. Light may soon dawn, especially if you approach the whole thing from a different angle.

• *Saturday 13 April* •

Your libido climbs up several notches from today and will remain very high until late May. It's a great opportunity to live up to your Scorpio reputation of being a red-hot lover! If you think that chance would be a fine thing, then start getting out and about and you might soon meet a new partner! This will also be a marvellous time to tackle subjects that you've considered to be taboo until now. You may feel brave enough to face them at long last, but try to respect the decision of anyone who doesn't want to follow your lead.

• *Sunday 14 April* •

It would be a shame to spend today in solitary splendour because you're in such a benevolent and sociable mood. You'll thoroughly enjoy being with like-minded people and will feel a really strong bond with them. If you meet someone new today it might be the start of an enjoyable association, even if it doesn't end in hearts and flowers. If you're already half of a happy couple, make a big fuss of your partner. They'll love you for it!

• *Monday 15 April* •

Your relationships continue to flourish and today it's your close and intimate partnerships that benefit the most. You're very keen to improve them in any way you can, but try not to be too forceful about this! Otherwise you may get irritated when partners don't reciprocate in the way you want. If you've been trying to sort out a financial muddle, give it another go now. You're absolutely determined to get things straightened out!

• *Tuesday 16 April* •

Turn your attention to your official money matters today. You're in a very sober and practical mood and you want to make sure you're doing everything possible to create a solid financial future. For instance, if you don't have a pension plan you might decide to start investigating your options, or you may want to find out about savings schemes that will eventually give you a nice nest egg.

• *Wednesday 17 April* •

Let your mind go on a journey today. You're in a very inquisitive mood and you won't be satisfied with glib or pat answers to your questions. You might become engrossed in a book that you can't put down or watch a TV programme that sets your mind racing with questions. Travel is another option now – even if you can't go on holiday at the moment you might start looking through brochures so you can find the perfect destination. It feels as though the world's your oyster.

• *Thursday 18 April* •

There's so much scope for muddles and misunderstandings today that you should be very careful when talking to others. Although you may think you're saying one thing, someone else may think you're saying something completely different. Before you know it, you'll be at cross purposes. This is not a good day to assume that you know what someone means. If you aren't sure, ask them. Be especially wary about reaching agreements because you may not have been given the whole story.

• *Friday 19 April* •

Get talking to someone who comes from a different background or culture from yours. The contrasts in your experiences will be a great talking point and may bring you together rather than pull you apart. There's a lot to learn about one another so you won't be lost for words! You may also hear from someone living in another country, and you'll be thrilled.

• *Saturday 20 April* •

The accent has been on your relationships recently and that's increased from today. During the next four weeks there will be times when you feel your identity is boosted by the people in your life and that you aren't realizing your full potential when you're on your own. Even if you go it alone for the rest of the year, this is a marvellous chance to get involved in some team work.

• *Sunday 21 April* •

Your sights are firmly set on work and other commitments today, especially if you're hoping to make up for lost time recently. However, it will be awfully easy to get bogged down in petty details or to pay too much attention to red tape, with the result that you don't seem to achieve very much at all. Older friends and relatives are difficult to deal with now because they're being critical or acerbic.

• *Monday 22 April* •

The atmosphere is much improved after yesterday's uncomfortable mood. You're feeling light-hearted and sociable, and if you suspect that you've upset someone you'll be quick to say sorry. Ideally, you should spend today in the company of others because you've got so much to contribute to conversations. Any form of group activity will suit you to a T, and you'll love being with kindred spirits.

• *Tuesday 23 April* •

A leisure activity is terrific fun today and helps to take you out of yourself. Every now and then it does you good to think about something that's completely removed from your everyday pursuits. If you've been wondering about how you can broaden your social life, you could hear now about a new group or organization that sounds as though it was made for you. Why not find out more about it?

• *Wednesday 24 April* •

A certain restlessness gets in the way of your relationship with you-know-who today. Perhaps you suddenly start to feel bored with them because you think they're being very predictable, or they're imposing restrictions on you that make you want to rebel. Alternatively, it's your partner who's trying to break away, and this will make you feel threatened and vulnerable. It may be a flash in the pan so try not to panic just yet.

• *Thursday 25 April* •

Your emotions take a very intense turn between today and the middle of May. You'll want to put a lot of effort into your close relationships and will expect to get a lot from them in return. If you've recently embarked on a new partnership, it will occupy almost all your emotional energy now and you may not have much time for anyone else. Even a long-standing relationship will go through a hectic phase now.

• *Friday 26 April* •

Prepare yourself for some nice surprises today. A loved one could give you an unexpected treat or spoil you rotten in some way. Or you may have a surprise visitor at home. Whatever happens out of the blue will be enjoyable. If you've been searching high and low for something that you've mislaid, you might find it where you least expect it now.

• *Saturday 27 April* •

Today's Full Moon is telling you that it's time to sort out any areas of your life that are currently in a muddle or need clearing up once and for all. Over the next two weeks you'll realize what you need to do and how to go about it. This will also be a marvellous chance to alter the current direction of your life if you think that's necessary. The sooner you make these changes, the sooner they'll take effect.

• *Sunday 28 April* •

Someone is feeling rather impatient today and it won't take much to make them fly off the handle. This will probably be over almost as soon as it begins but it will be unsettling and you won't enjoy it very much. Watch out if you're the one who's feeling ratty and sharp-tongued because you may say things that you'll regret once you've simmered down.

• *Monday 29 April* •

A discussion or conversation leads to entrenched views today. Everyone concerned seems determined to dig their heels in and refuse to accept anyone else's opinion, and that goes for you too! Even if you're convinced that you're in the right, it won't hurt to listen to other people's viewpoints. You may learn something to your advantage and you might also realize that you haven't got all the answers after all!

• *Tuesday 30 April* •

Official finances, such as your tax affairs, need careful scrutiny between now and early July. Go over them carefully, seeing where improvements can be made. If you think you need expert advice, this is definitely the time to ask for it. You'll also enjoy doing some research on your own because you'll gain tremendous satisfaction from digging away to get at the truth. It's the same story in your close relationships – if you think someone is holding out on you, you'll be determined to worm the truth out of them.

MAY AT A GLANCE

Love	♥ ♥ ♥ ♥ ♥
Money	£ $ £ $ £
Career	💻
Health	☼ ☼

• *Wednesday 1 May* •

You start the month unsure of yourself, and it's disconcerting. For some reason you are feeling uncertain and undecided. It won't help that someone may be trying to undermine your confidence, even if they do it in very subtle ways. You may also be lacking in energy so it's a struggle to achieve very much. This isn't a good day to take important decisions about your home and family because so much is up in the air. The picture will be clearer on Friday.

• *Thursday 2 May* •

This is a day for reflection rather than action. In fact, if you do try to get anything new off the ground you will be stymied and feel as though you're losing a battle. Things simply won't go right and there won't be much you can do about it. Instead, channel your energies into reviewing your current situation. It's also good for reading through any written work you are involved in and checking that it's up to scratch.

• *Friday 3 May* •

If you were hampered by Wednesday's indecision you are now in a much better position to take action. It may help to pick the brains of the other people involved or to ask the advice of someone who you always respect. This is also a good day to pay attention to your domestic finances and to make sure everything is ticking over nicely. You know what they say about a stitch in time . . .

• *Saturday 4 May* •

You're very decisive today and anything you do will make a tremendous impact on everyone around you. You certainly shouldn't underestimate yourself. It's an excellent day to carry on where you left off yesterday in sorting out your finances, and perhaps to broaden your scope to include joint and official money matters. For instance, if you know you need to take action about your tax affairs, do so now.

• *Sunday 5 May* •

Anything goes today, especially on the home front. Someone may drop in unexpectedly or one of the family may deliver a bolt from the blue. The chances are that you'll be intrigued by all this, once the excitement has died down. If you've been spending too much time in one place recently it will start to get to you today and you'll long for a change of scene.

• *Monday 6 May* •

There's no need to worry about the Monday morning blues because you're in a very jolly mood. In fact, you're keen to get as much enjoyment out of the day as possible, especially if you can be sociable at the same time. Travel plans also appeal now and if you've been trying to talk yourself out of booking a holiday, you may have to succumb to temptation any minute now! Even a short break will do you good.

• *Tuesday 7 May* •

Once again, you're in a very sunny mood and you want to have a good time. This shouldn't be a problem since it looks as though everyone is only too happy to oblige. You're popular and for good reason! You're also feeling confident, so it's a great chance to break the ice with someone or phone up a casual friend and suggest an evening out. You're very keen to increase your links with others now.

• *Wednesday 8 May* •

Go carefully today because it will be awfully easy to develop a one-track mind and lose all sense of reality. You have strong will power at the best of times but it's even more pronounced now, and you'll do your best to get people to go along with what you want. But be careful because this tenacity could easily lead to a bloody-mindedness that is off-putting to others and makes them treat you with suspicion.

• *Thursday 9 May* •

Emotions run high today, especially if you didn't get what you wanted yesterday. Rather than blaze a trail that ensures you get your own way, try to be more delicate about announcing your needs. You should also be careful when dealing with emotional matters that you don't become single-minded about getting what you want. Watch out, too, for a possible jealous streak. Not an easy day!

• *Friday 10 May* •

Matters come to a head today and it will involve a lot of emotional energy on your part. If you've been stewing for the past couple of days, you'll now want to let off steam in no uncertain manner. But there are good points about the day as well because you may have a very intense encounter with you-know-who, and it will remind them that everything they've heard about Scorpio being the sign of sex is true. It's enough to make the wallpaper peel!

• *Saturday 11 May* •

You're in a much more cheery and easy-going mood than you've been for days, and it comes as quite a relief – not only to you but also to the people around you. It's a super day for doing something that will help you to relax, and also apologize to loved ones if you think it's necessary. If you don't have anything planned this weekend, how about taking off on the spur of the moment, whether you go for the day or the whole weekend?

• *Sunday 12 May* •

Today's New Moon affects your relationships for the coming two weeks. This is a fabulous chance to attend to any partnerships that have been languishing recently for want of attention. For instance, if you've been feeling guilty about neglecting someone in your life, make up for it now. Equally, if you've fallen out with a partner this is a good chance to make amends. Someone might enter your life now, in which case you'll be excited by their arrival.

• *Monday 13 May* •

It's very hard to settle down to anything for long because there are so many irritating interruptions. You also have the uncomfortable experience of quickly becoming bored with whatever you're doing but not knowing what to do instead. It won't help that certain people are being recalcitrant or obstructive, and you feel as though you're beating your head against a brick wall. Calm down – it will soon blow over.

• *Tuesday 14 May* •

It won't take much to make you lose your temper today, especially if it seems that a loved one is taking you for granted. There may also be problems because of someone's jealous or possessive behaviour. Try not to let these escalate into massive rifts, even if part of you wants to take a stand. Is it really worth it? If you're sorting out an official financial matter, you'll get very impatient if people seem to drag their feet.

• *Wednesday 15 May* •

The accent has been on close partnerships and your joint finances recently so it isn't exactly good news to know that you'll have problems in communicating on these subjects over the next three weeks. People may get the wrong end of the stick, whether accidentally or deliberately. There could also be muddles connected with a pension policy, insurance claim or your tax situation, so be very careful.

• *Thursday 16 May* •

You've got the travel bug today. Whether you go on a mental or physical journey, the last thing you want is to feel you're stagnating or just marking time. Anything that seems exciting or presents you with a challenge is perfect for you now, and you'll jump at the chance to prove yourself. It's also a good day for taking a mini gamble, although you shouldn't risk anything you can't afford to lose.

• *Friday 17 May* •

You're determined to make the most of the day and to enjoy it as much as possible. This means you'll be able to laugh off anything that would usually make you angry or irritated, and you'll also manage to lighten the atmosphere around you. If you need to talk to someone and hope you'll catch them in a good mood, you shouldn't have any problems with them today.

• *Saturday 18 May* •

You feel as though you're being swayed in several different directions today, and it will end up being very confusing. If you need to reach a decision about your home life or a career matter, you'll keep vacillating between your different options until you don't know whether you're coming or going.

Perhaps you should put the decision on hold until you're more sure of yourself? You don't want to have to backtrack at a later date.

• *Sunday 19 May* •

Restless feelings overtake you today, making it hard to get on with anything for long. You may also be in one of those difficult moods where you instinctively disagree with everything you're told, even though you recognize the sense in it. You're also highly sensitive to any suspicion that someone is taking advantage of you or wasting your time. It's a combustible combination and could easily end in raised voices and hurt feelings.

• *Monday 20 May* •

The emotional atmosphere has been very tense recently but there is some light relief from today because you're very keen to broaden your horizons and have a more open mind about your relationships. Between now and mid-June you may surprise someone by having a complete change of heart over something that you've been very dogmatic about in the past. There's also a chance that you'll lose your heart to something or someone with international connections.

• *Tuesday 21 May* •

If you've been wondering how to improve your relationships, start examining them in more detail than usual. Between now and late June you'll really benefit from looking at all the ins and outs of your partnerships. Think about your motives in knowing people and what you hope to gain from your relationship. What, in turn, do people gain from knowing you? You may even be inspired to discuss this with certain people and it will teach you a lot about one another.

• *Wednesday 22 May* •

You're in a very open-hearted mood today and there's nothing you'll like better than being with some of the special people in your life. You want to make a fuss of them and remind them of the place they occupy in your heart. There's a lot of goodwill directed towards you at the moment, so use this chance to get on the right side of someone who hasn't been very friendly recently.

• *Thursday 23 May* •

Luck is definitely on your side today but it could come from an unexpected source. Someone may act like your guardian angel, coming to your aid just when you need it. If you've been waiting nervously for news of a benefit or allowance that you think you may be entitled to, there could be good tidings today. You are also in a charitable mood and will take pleasure from doing things that help others.

• *Friday 24 May* •

It's no good paying much attention to a relative today because they're making very little sense. However, before you jump to the conclusion that it must be their fault, bear in mind that you may be equally to blame. Perhaps you're not listening to what they're saying and are actually only hearing what you want to hear? You may also be feeling defensive about the subject under discussion, so that you want to gloss over it as soon as possible.

• *Saturday 25 May* •

Anything that smacks of adventure is perfect just now! You're in the mood for a challenge today and you want to make the most of it. You certainly won't be put off by any apparent disadvantages or reasons for playing safe. All the same, try not to be foolhardy or to take risks that you would normally shy away from. It's all very well being a daredevil but you don't want to kick yourself for it later.

• *Sunday 26 May* •

You get the best of both worlds today. You're able to assert your emotional independence when necessary without upsetting anyone or making them think you don't love them any more. This will be quite a feat so you deserve to pat yourself on the back. It's also a good day to swing into action on the domestic front, especially if you've had to hang fire recently. Suddenly, you know exactly what you want to achieve and how to go about it.

• *Monday 27 May* •

Someone's very chatty today! They're being a lot more communicative than usual and it seems they're also keen to talk about subjects that are usually kept under wraps or considered taboo. Grab this chance to talk things through, especially if that means you can clear up lingering problems or discuss topics that have been nagging away at you recently. It's also a good day for discussing intimate subjects, such as your sex life, in an objective way.

• *Tuesday 28 May* •

You're fired with enthusiasm for life from today, and you'll want to put as much energy into it as possible during the coming few weeks. In fact, between now and mid-July is marvellous for focusing on activities that you've never done before. You're feeling brave enough to give them a go and you don't want to feel that you've let yourself down. Equally, if life has thrown down the gauntlet at your feet, you're now determined to pick it up and accept the challenge. You won't be beaten!

• *Wednesday 29 May* •

It's a day for having fun, even if you have to fit in some work as well. You're keen to go on a mini adventure, so what do you have in mind? Anything connected with travel is a good option now because you long to spread your wings. You might receive a tempting invitation to go and stay with someone or maybe you want to invite them to stay with you. You're also very taken by someone who comes from another country or culture from yours.

• *Thursday 30 May* •

If you want to organize your domestic budget in a better way, have a crack at it today. You're in a practical and organized mood, and you want to get things sorted out in the most sensible way you can think of. If you're fed up with doing all the work around the house yourself, how about discussing it with the rest of the family and seeing if you can devise a rota so that everyone does their share?

• *Friday 31 May* •

Your idea of fun is to be with some of your nearest and dearest today. You'll enjoy knowing that you don't have to make a special effort with them and that they're happy to let you be yourself. You don't expect loved ones to put on any airs and graces either, so it will be a relaxed atmosphere all round. If you're considering moving house, the idea will be even more appealing than usual now.

JUNE AT A GLANCE

Love	♥ ♥ ♥ ♥ ♥
Money	£ $ £ $ £
Career	💻 💻 💻 💻
Health	☼ ☼

• *Saturday 1 June* •

You're very keen to put yourself out in order to help others today. As far as you're concerned right now, their needs are greater than yours and you're very happy to take a back seat while they bask in all the attention. You're feeling especially warm towards members of the clan and close friends who you consider to be family. You feel as though there's almost nothing you wouldn't do for them. Even so, be wary about making promises that you may not be able to keep.

• *Sunday 2 June* •

You're in a fantastic mood today – outgoing, energetic and ebullient. You're also determined not to be fazed by whatever comes along, but it doesn't look as though you have any need to worry because life treats you gently today. You're very taken by the prospect of travel, especially if it's for pleasure. You also want to respond to someone's dare or challenge, and you'll give it your best shot.

• *Monday 3 June* •

Life is a party today! You're eager to get involved in anything that's enjoyable and fun. If you've had your eye on someone from another country recently, sparks will fly between you today and your relationship may enter a completely new phase as a result. This doesn't have to be a love affair – it might be an enjoyable friendship. You might also fall head over heels for a course or study that captures your interest and gives you a new outlook on the world.

• *Tuesday 4 June* •

Take care if you're at work today because you won't appreciate anything that feels like a restriction or limitation. In fact, your instinct will be to rebel against it as powerfully as you can manage. Unfortunately, this won't go down very well in some quarters. For instance, if you're expected to put in some overtime to help out a colleague, or you can't take any time off at the moment because you're so busy, your mutinous attitude will raise someone's hackles.

• *Wednesday 5 June* •

If you want to sort out something connected with your salary or wages, tackle it today while you're in the right frame of mind. What's more, the powers that be will be helpful and reasonable. Alternatively, you might be on the receiving end of a bonus or perk from a satisfied customer or a grateful boss. It's also a good day to spend money on items that will boost your well-being in some way.

• *Thursday 6 June* •

Once again, there are difficulties when dealing with colleagues and bosses. If you're still simmering about what happened on Tuesday, you'll get steamed up all over again now. But does it have to be like this? A little give and take on both sides will make all the difference and will also make it apparent that you're prepared to compromise where necessary, even though you will stand firm on some of your complaints.

• *Friday 7 June* •

Turn your attention to your finances today if you want to get to the bottom of a mystery. You'll soon discover what's gone wrong because you won't rest until you get the answers you want. Woe betide anyone who tries to pull the wool over your eyes or use delaying tactics because you'll soon make short shrift of them. All the same, don't be ruthless if it isn't completely justified or you'll set someone against you.

• *Saturday 8 June* •

If you've been getting fed up with silly mistakes in your finances recently, you'll be glad to know that things start to return to normal from today. They may not automatically sort themselves out, though, so some diligence may be required on your part. Whatever else you do today, try to fit in something sociable at some point, especially if it's with people who always make you laugh or help you to see the lighter side of life.

• *Sunday 9 June* •

You're capable of very deep thinking and some profound observations today. You're prepared to look life straight in the eye, even if you don't always like what you see. This is a marvellous day for some soul-searching because you're unflinching when examining your motives and scrutinizing your most intimate relationships. This may not be an entirely comfortable experience but it will certainly be a rewarding one.

• *Monday 10 June* •

Right on cue, today's powerful Eclipsed New Moon underlines the conclusions you reached yesterday. If you've decided that you need to make major changes to a close relationship, the rest of the month is the perfect time to set the ball rolling. For instance, you may realize that a certain relationship is well worth salvaging, even though it's been going through a rocky phase lately.

• *Tuesday 11 June* •

After a sobering couple of days, life gives you plenty to smile about again. There are lots of surprises in the pipeline and they'll keep you on your toes. One of the family does something that makes you think twice, although for all the right reasons. If you've been thinking about changing the décor at home or altering the look of the garden, you'll have some good ideas today.

• *Wednesday 12 June* •

You're in an adventurous mood today and you want to do things that reflect this. One thing you don't want to do is to play it safe or hedge your bets. In fact, the very idea probably appals you! Although you want to stick your neck out, try not to do it with such enthusiasm that you end up getting into trouble or putting both feet in it. However, anything that requires courage will benefit from today's influences.

• *Thursday 13 June* •

Once again, you're keen to go the whole hog and you don't want to do things by halves. You'll jump at any chance to follow up opportunities and if someone makes you a good offer now you won't be able to refuse it. Travel beckons, too, even if you can't do anything about it at the moment. At least think about where you'll go on holiday when you get the chance.

• *Friday 14 June* •

Between now and the middle of July you'll want to make a big effort to get on the right side of people of power and influence. This might mean overlooking recent problems between you and an older relative and restoring the harmony between you. Or it might mean being extra friendly to a boss or superior.

There's a chance that you could be strongly attracted to someone in a position of power, in which case you must be honest with yourself about why you're so drawn to them.

• *Saturday 15 June* •

If you think you've sorted out your recent financial problems but you want to make sure, go over everything in detail today. For instance, you might want to check your credit card balance to make sure that a payment went through, or find out how a current investment is performing. It's also a nice day for chatting to someone you respect and getting to know them as a fellow human being rather than a person on a pedestal.

• *Sunday 16 June* •

Your mind is working well today, especially when it comes to your goals and long-term ambitions. Spend some time thinking about what you want to do next in your current job or how you can improve your social status. You might also benefit from someone's advice, so don't be shy about telling them what you're planning and asking them for their opinion.

• *Monday 17 June* •

If you want a nice, quiet life today you would be wise to keep finances and friends at arm's length. Otherwise all hell will be let loose when someone becomes envious of another person's good fortune. For example, someone's nose may be put out of joint because you've just bought something that they can't afford. If you're arranging a forthcoming social event, there could be bad feeling about the cost, especially if someone thinks it's all too expensive. Put it on hold for the time being.

• *Tuesday 18 June* •

It's another difficult day and once again money is the root of the problem. This time, you should be very wary of lending anything that you want to be returned because there's a chance you may never see it again. Are you quite sure that you want to part with it? You should also be careful about asking for a loan yourself because you won't get the answer you were hoping for. It certainly isn't a good day to apply for a loan from a financial organization.

• *Wednesday 19 June* •

Just when your chin was starting to hit the floor after the recent gloomy days, your spirits start to rise again. Even if life is being very difficult at the moment, you're feeling much more positive about your prospects today. You might see a glimmer of light at the end of the tunnel or you may feel able to take all these disappointments and setbacks on the chin. If you have a religious or spiritual belief, this will give you added support now.

• *Thursday 20 June* •

If you held back from applying for a loan at the start of the week, your patience is being rewarded because this is a much more auspicious day for getting involved in all financial matters. You may even find, much to your delight, that someone goes out of their way to accommodate you or make life easier in some way. If you're currently involved in plans about moving house, stand by for surprise developments now. Things may start to happen rather fast!

• *Friday 21 June* •

Your horizons start to broaden from today, and over the next four weeks you'll want to get as much out of life as possible. You certainly won't be content to settle for the status quo because you're beginning to see the bigger picture and have a good idea of what you might be able to achieve over the coming months. If you're wondering where on earth 2002 is going because the days are passing so quickly, you won't want to waste a moment longer than necessary. Strike while the iron's hot!

• *Saturday 22 June* •

Life takes some unexpected turns today and they won't exactly meet with your approval. For a start, you may have to deal with last-minute events and changes of plan, and these will throw your schedule out of whack. You may also have to cope with someone who is apparently doing their level best to be disruptive and awkward. But before you point the finger of blame at others, do make sure you haven't fallen into this trap yourself! It's easier than you think right now.

• *Sunday 23 June* •

Although you're usually almost painfully realistic, today finds you in a very idealistic mood. You're turning a blind eye to unpleasant facts and doing your best to sweep them under the nearest carpet. Although this may not seem to matter much at the moment, it won't do you any good in the long run because it will mean you aren't prepared for the disappointment or disillusionment that arrives at a later date and causes the scales to fall from your eyes with a mighty clatter.

• *Monday 24 June* •

Have a think about ways to improve your home and family life today. Maybe you know exactly what to do, especially if it involves lending someone your emotional or practical support? If you aren't so sure about how to make things better, listen to your intuition because it could give you some excellent insights. It will also help to talk to the rest of the family and see what they think. You're a good listener right now.

• *Tuesday 25 June* •

You're in reflective mood today and will enjoy mulling things over whenever you get the chance. You're especially keen to think about close relatives and neighbourhood issues. For example, if things have been dicey recently with someone who you see on a daily basis, consider how you can improve matters and also find out what's at the root of the problem. If you've got some free time, you'll thoroughly enjoy curling up with a favourite magazine or a gripping book.

• *Wednesday 26 June* •

Gently does it! You're raring to go and you're so full of enthusiasm that you've got a tendency to rush into things without thinking them through first. This could have disastrous results, perhaps with you dropping a clanger because you speak before you think, or making a hash of something because you're trying to cut corners. Be careful when talking to someone who's often rather huffy because you may inadvertently say the wrong thing and not even notice.

• *Thursday 27 June* •

It's been a rather mixed June and you're reaching the stage where you desperately need to take things easy. This is the perfect day to do it, provided you get the chance! Why not pull up a deckchair and relax in the garden, or simply enjoy pottering around at home? Something else that appeals now is doing some cooking, especially if you're making some treats or experimenting with the ingredients in the fridge.

• *Friday 28 June* •

Turn your attention to your finances today because you'll make a lot of headway. It's a super day for making careful decisions about investments and other ways to make your money work for you. If a powerful rapport has been building between you and someone with a lot of clout or authority, your relationship will go through an important phase today that brings you closer together. If you suspect this is love, you'll feel powerless to resist it. And you don't want to, either!

• *Saturday 29 June* •

There's a lot of enjoyment to be had today and you're determined to make the most of it. Everyone you meet is in a good mood so it's easy to get along with them. If someone offers you an opportunity you'll soon jump at it. The travel bug bites now, making you eager for pastures new. You can't think of anything nicer than packing your suitcase and jumping on an aeroplane. Is it possible, or is it nothing more than a pipe dream right now?

• *Sunday 30 June* •

Any hint of jealousy or possessiveness will get a very severe response today, so think twice before behaving as though someone is your personal property. Unfortunately, your natural Scorpio tendency towards possessiveness is activated now, especially if you're feeling emotionally vulnerable or you're worried that a certain person seems to be slipping away from you. Clinging to them is the surest way to repel them at the moment.

JULY AT A GLANCE

Love	♥ ♥
Money	£ $ £
Career	💻 💻 💻 💻 💻
Health	☼

• *Monday 1 July* •

It's one of those days when you feel ready for anything! You're in a happy-go-lucky mood and you want to get the very best from the day. If you've got to do something today that makes your heart sink whenever you think about it, adopting a positive attitude to it will make all the difference. You may find that it wasn't nearly as bad as you had imagined. You might even enjoy it!

• *Tuesday 2 July* •

You feel burdened by hard work today and it seems as though you'll never get through all the tasks lined up for you at the moment. Unfortunately, this is almost guaranteed to make you feel tired and listless. It may also make you rather irritable and you certainly won't be happy if anyone asks you to do them a favour. Try not to bite their head off!

• *Wednesday 3 July* •

You're feeling energetic and buzzy today, especially if you're faced with anything remotely resembling a challenge. Whereas yesterday you would probably have wanted to ignore it completely, today it's grist to your mill and you can't wait to tackle it. In fact, any activity that allows you to stretch yourself and discover hidden talents is ideal for you now. It's even better if it involves some physical exercise.

• *Thursday 4 July* •

If you're currently trying to sort out a financial mystery connected with your salary or wages, it takes another surprising turn today. Don't worry, because it won't be anything serious, but it will remind you not to take anything or anyone for granted at the moment. Keep your eyes peeled for attractive customers or dazzling colleagues today because someone could easily make your knees go wobbly.

• *Friday 5 July* •

You're very keen to get on well with everyone today, even if that means humouring them slightly or letting them have their own way. It's not that you want to make yourself out to be a doormat or to send them the message that they can always be selfish – it's simply that you can't see the point in arguing over silly trifles. Your sense of humour won't allow you to be petty or small-minded at the moment.

• *Saturday 6 July* •

If you're currently trying to find a way to finance a domestic plan or home improvement and you haven't got very far yet, think it through again today. If possible, approach it from another angle and see if light dawns as a result. A family get-together promises to be highly enjoyable now, and you might even see a new side to someone's character. It will be a revelation and will endear them to you.

• *Sunday 7 July* •

You're filled with curiosity about the world from today, and this thirst for knowledge won't leave you until the middle of the month. Until then, you'll thoroughly enjoy cramming your head with facts. You may even decide that you want to start an evening class or enrol in a correspondence course, simply for the pleasure of giving your brain some exercise. Start considering which options might be open to you.

• *Monday 8 July* •

Pay close attention to your finances today, especially when it comes to sorting out such things as your taxes, VAT and other official money matters. Even if you've been putting something off because you can't bear the thought of it, you'll now be able to bite the bullet and face up to the facts. If anything, you're erring on the side of caution and pessimism, so if you're assessing your current situation you may take a rather gloomy view of it.

• *Tuesday 9 July* •

Life has some interesting surprises up its sleeve today. Someone dear to your heart may want to show their independence in dramatic ways, especially if they feel their wings are clipped at the moment. For instance, one of the family may talk about leaving home, provoking a lot of upset in the process. If you're faced by someone who wants to fly the nest or lead a more independent life, it won't help if you try to cling on to them. They may react by being really rebellious.

• *Wednesday 10 July* •

Today's New Moon is just what you need! It's the clarion call that signals it's time to start broadening your life in all directions. You're suddenly not content to deal with the status quo any longer, you want to branch out into pastures new. Life seems full of enticing adventures that you can't wait to try. You may even decide that your current mode of living is far too restrictive and you owe it to yourself to expand your horizons.

• *Thursday 11 July* •

Once again you're determined to spread your wings and fly. Travel is certainly a very tempting option right now, and if you haven't yet booked up a holiday this year it will be almost impossible to resist going into your nearest travel agent or finding a last-minute bargain on the Internet. You're also very keen on taking up any challenges that arrive now, and the more testing they are the better. You're determined to prove that you're no coward!

• *Friday 12 July* •

Tread carefully today because a certain person isn't making nearly as much sense as they think they are. They may have got their wires crossed or they may be living in cloud cuckoo land and be completely out of touch with reality. You'll know this is happening if they're wrapped up in the past and can only talk about the good old days, or if they're making wild guesses and then convincing themselves that these are solid facts.

• *Saturday 13 July* •

Your ambitions are fired from today, and they'll continue to propel you through the next six weeks at the speed of light. You've got a very good idea of what you want to achieve now and you're utterly determined that nothing and no one will stand in your way. This is a marvellous chance to push yourself forward, but mind how you go. If you give someone the impression that you're ruthless, they may see you as a threat and try to trip you up.

• *Sunday 14 July* •

Life is full of enjoyment today. You're in a very outgoing mood so you won't want to spend much time alone if you can possibly avoid it. It's a super day for being with people on the same wavelength as you because you'll thoroughly enjoy their company. You'll also like talking to them about virtually any subject under the sun. If you're involved in some sort of group activity today, it will go really well.

• *Monday 15 July* •

If you need to stand up for yourself, it will be easy to defend your interests today. What's more, you'll do it without making a big song and dance, which will go down well all round. It's a good day for being busy at work because you have plenty of stamina and enthusiasm. However, it will be best if you can work by yourself. You won't have much patience for anyone who's being a slowcoach.

• *Tuesday 16 July* •

It's one of those days when it's awfully easy to speak out of turn. You're in a very quick-witted frame of mind, which may mean you blurt things out that are better left unsaid. Yet you'll only realize this when it's too late. Be very careful when talking about things that are meant to be a secret. You may think you're dropping subtle hints but you may be revealing more than you intended.

• *Wednesday 17 July* •

If you accidentally let the cat out of the bag yesterday, or someone betrayed one of your secrets, you can expect plenty of repercussions today. You may be hopping mad with the person who blabbed, or they may have something to say to you on the subject. Once again, you should choose your words carefully. Be especially wary about discussing topics connected with politics, the environment or religion because it will be horribly easy to offend someone.

• *Thursday 18 July* •

How are you feeling? Do you feel as though someone's pulled out a plug and all your energy has evaporated? It's highly likely that you're feeling dispirited and demoralized today, and it won't help if someone is doing their best to point out your failings. You're ultra-sensitive to what others think of you now, and any hint of criticism or unfriendliness will cut you to the quick.

• *Friday 19 July* •

You've bounced back after yesterday's downcast mood and once again you're firing on all cylinders. Keep your eyes peeled for a wonderful opportunity that comes along now. It may involve an act of faith or a leap of the imagination, but if your gut instincts tell you that it's worth a punt then you should certainly pay attention to them. Chances like these don't come along every day, so don't let this one slip through your fingers.

• *Saturday 20 July* •

Once again, luck is on your side. In fact, things are working in your favour even more than they were yesterday, and you're convinced that you're sitting pretty. You may well be right, but try not to be so confident that you take foolish risks or imagine that things will fall into your lap without any effort on your part. Anything connected with travel, further education, politics or religion will go swimmingly now.

• *Sunday 21 July* •

Your mind has been awakened this July and you're now casting around for ways to increase its scope even further. Spend some time thinking about your job prospects and long-term goals. Would they be improved if you could add another string to your bow? Maybe you should learn a new skill or brush up an old technique? Start considering your options during the next two weeks. It will also be an excellent time to pick the brains of people whose opinion you respect or who have the sort of experience you will benefit from.

• *Monday 22 July* •

You're in a very meditative mood today and nothing will give you more pleasure than to spend some time mulling things over. You may want to write down your thoughts or you might discuss them with a close relative. This is also a good day for taking part in local activities, such as a get-together with the neighbours or attending a residents' meeting. You'll enjoy feeling that you're part of a group.

• *Tuesday 23 July* •

Lately you've started to feel quite ambitious, and you're even more determined to succeed from today. In fact, during the coming month you will want to devote a lot of time and effort to getting on in the world and being seen to be a success. For instance, you may decide to stand for election to something that you believe in, or you'll apply for promotion if you think you deserve it. You will certainly be more in the spotlight than usual.

• *Wednesday 24 July* •

Today's Full Moon reminds you that even if your sights are set on improving your career prospects or nailing an ambition, you must also pay attention to what's going on closer to home. Between now and early August, members of the family will be very miffed if they think they're being neglected in favour of your work or your long-term aims. You may also have to make some difficult decisions about the welfare of one of the family, especially if they aren't able to take care of themselves.

• *Thursday 25 July* •

Your mind is working in double-quick time today. There are no flies on you! If you're taking part in a brainstorming session, you'll come up with the answers long before anyone else. However, make sure you don't cut corners, even though this is a temping option right now, because that may lead to embarrassing mistakes or accusations of not doing the job properly. You may also be rather hot-headed or outspoken at times.

• *Friday 26 July* •

Do your best to avoid making commitments or signing on any dotted lines today. Even if someone isn't deliberately being deceitful, they may still give you misleading information or forget to tell you something vital. If you have no option but to sign a contract today, make sure you read the small print and don't make assumptions because these may have nothing to do with the facts. Try to focus on as many details as possible and don't be shy about asking penetrating or awkward questions.

• *Saturday 27 July* •

Money comes between you and a certain person today. It might cause bad feeling, with one of you being envious of what you see as the other one's good fortune. There may also be a certain amount of emotional blackmail going on, with someone dropping heavy hints about things they would like to happen. Be very careful about implying things yourself without being more explicit because it won't go down very well.

• *Sunday 28 July* •

You feel as though you're fighting a losing battle today. Someone may demoralize you so you begin to doubt what you're doing, or you might start to run out of energy so you end up running on empty. If your job has been very demanding recently, this is a day to forget all about it and recuperate as much as possible. Even if you were to do some work you would probably take much longer than usual and that would be a waste of time, so give yourself a break!

• *Monday 29 July* •

If you're a typical Scorpio you have a mind like a razor, and today is a good opportunity to put it to the test. You'll be able to think things through in tremendous detail, especially when it comes to examining your finances or your career prospects. In fact, you'll be so thorough that you'll leave no stone unturned and no questions unanswered. Anyone influential or powerful who happens to be watching you will be most impressed.

• *Tuesday 30 July* •

This is the perfect day for rolling up your sleeves and getting down to some work. You're keen to get ahead and also to do a good job, and you shouldn't have any problems at all. If you're going to an interview or meeting, you'll come across as someone who knows their own mind and who isn't going to be pushed around, yet you'll stop short of being too dogmatic or forceful. It sounds as though you've got the best of both worlds!

• *Wednesday 31 July* •

If you've been promising yourself that you're going to lose weight, give up smoking, cut down on alcohol or make any other changes that will improve your health, your good intentions will soon fall by the wayside today. They all feel too much like hard work and you really can't be bothered with them. Instead, you want to indulge yourself whenever you get the chance. How about saying goodbye to July by going out for a drink or a meal?

AUGUST AT A GLANCE

Love	♥ ♥
Money	£ $
Career	🖳 🖳 🖳 🖳 🖳
Health	☼ ☼

• *Thursday 1 August* •

You're already thinking carefully about pushing ahead with your long-term plans and goals, and from today you're even more interested in making a name for yourself. Play your cards right over the next few months and you'll have some really lucky breaks. You may even make tremendous headway that seems unthinkable at the moment. If your career is connected with travel, education or the law, you may be about to hit the jackpot!

• *Friday 2 August* •

There have been several occasions recently when you've had reason to doubt what certain people are telling you. Today, you're once again unsure of where you stand. You may also begin to wonder whether you've got the facts straight and whether you are also guilty of getting in a muddle. However, before you start heaping coals of fire on your head, consider that you may be taking too gloomy a view of the entire situation. You may also be listening to someone who will benefit in some way from denting your confidence.

• *Saturday 3 August* •

You're in a very organized frame of mind today, which is just what you need if you want to sort out your finances or get down to plenty of work. Whatever you want to achieve now, you won't be happy until you've got it under your belt. This is also a good day to think carefully about your job prospects. It may help to talk to someone whose opinion you always respect.

• *Sunday 4 August* •

The last thing you want today is to be taken for granted, or to have to deal with someone who thinks they know you better than you know yourself. This sort of behaviour will soon have you at screaming pitch, and you won't be very diplomatic when voicing your objections! You may also talk to someone who's being completely dogmatic and who refuses to shift their opinions one jot. It will be a waste of time and effort trying to get them to change their mind.

• *Monday 5 August* •

You're in a very lively and upbeat mood today, and if this is the start of your working week you'll want to give it your best shot. However, it's best if you've got something nice to look forward to now because the anticipation will keep you going through the day. If you've been meaning to buy something new for your home, have a look around the shops: you could spot the very thing you're after.

• *Tuesday 6 August* •

You're being very forceful today, yet luckily you manage to stop short of being overwhelming. This is the perfect opportunity to tell someone what you think, especially if it's something that means a lot to you. You won't pull your punches and you won't waste your time talking about inconsequentials. People will sit up and take notice, so make the most of your current ability to impress others.

• *Wednesday 7 August* •

Romance is one of the main themes of the next four weeks. If you've set your sights on a certain person, they may soon make it plain that they're equally smitten. However, don't be surprised if you have to keep the whole affair under wraps for the time being. It will be important for you to have a little time to yourself between now and early September, and you'll really value these interludes of peace and quiet.

• *Thursday 8 August* •

Today's New Moon fires you with fresh enthusiasm to make a big splash in your career and with your public reputation. Over the next two weeks you might get the chance to be in the limelight, or you may finally hear whether your recent efforts have paid off. For instance, if you've been hoping to be promoted or given a pay rise, you'll soon discover whether you're going to be lucky.

• *Friday 9 August* •

Anything or anyone that threatens to tie you down or restrict your freedom will soon have you fuming today. You can't abide the thought of others telling you what to do, which may cause problems if your boss or a superior is issuing orders. You may be tempted to tell them what to do with them! However, you would be wise to think twice before making any challenging remarks or blotting your copybook. It will count against you.

• *Saturday 10 August* •

There's no stopping you today! You're full of energy and you know exactly what you want to achieve. What's more, you're keen to stick your neck out if necessary – you certainly won't want to give the impression of being shy and retiring! If you're attending an important interview or meeting you'll feel confident, but try not to overdo it and give the impression that you're cocky or think you have all the answers.

• *Sunday 11 August* •

If this is your rest day, you'll thoroughly enjoy having some time to yourself. Maybe you should take the phone off the hook and ignore the doorbell? However, it would be a shame to spend the entire day without making contact with anyone else because someone will be very helpful and encouraging. They may give you some useful information or show that they have your best interests at heart. You may even wonder if they're your guardian angel in disguise.

• *Monday 12 August* •

Once again, you'll be happiest if you can be left to your own devices at some point today. You may have to explain to disgruntled loved ones that you aren't being unfriendly, you simply need to be allowed to potter around by yourself. Listening to some favourite music on your headphones rather than watching the TV with everyone else might do the trick, or having a long soak in the bath while reading a favourite magazine.

• *Tuesday 13 August* •

If there have been problems between you and a certain someone recently, you'll be at pains to put the entire episode behind you today. You realize that life is too short to bear grudges and, besides, you really can't be bothered! There are so many more important things to think about! Someone in a position of authority or power is looking favourably in your direction right now, so let them know that you're interested in receiving their help and attention.

• *Wednesday 14 August* •

If you're currently in the middle of a home improvement scheme or you're trying to organize a house move, be very careful about what people do and don't say today. Someone who seems absent-minded may actually be trying to gloss over some difficult facts that they would rather keep you in the dark about. You may also come into contact with a member of the family who's living in the past.

• *Thursday 15 August* •

Patience may be a virtue but it's in very short supply today. It may even be almost non-existent, especially where your dealings with a certain person are concerned. This person will push you to the limits, yet there may be good reasons why you can't lose your temper with them. For instance, they may be your boss or an older relative, and you just can't bring yourself to yell at them. However, you can still make it plain that you aren't pleased.

• *Friday 16 August* •

Even though Scorpio isn't usually a sign associated with idealism, you're highly likely to put someone on a lofty pedestal today. You think they can do no wrong, and that may be true at the moment but don't kid yourself that this person is a saint in human form or a cut above the rest of us. If you think like this, you'll be very disappointed later on when they turn out to be as flawed as everyone else.

• *Saturday 17 August* •

You've got a yearning to spend some money today, especially on items that will boost your ego or make you look good. If you're currently trying to track down clothes for work, this is a good day to see what's on offer. It's also good for buying any items that will help you in your job or get you into the public eye, whether they're as minor as a box of paperclips or as major as a new computer.

• *Sunday 18 August* •

Try to make the most of today whenever you get the chance. Curl up in a chair with the Sunday papers and read them from cover to cover, or lose yourself in a book that you simply can't put down. It's a super day for using your mind and thinking things over. You don't want to take action, however, because you're quite happy being contemplative at the moment.

• *Monday 19 August* •

If you spent yesterday cogitating and making plans, you're now starting to feel keen to get things off the ground. You're in a very practical and organized mood today, and you'll be even more efficient if you can plan your strategy in advance to avoid wasting time or doing something twice. If you're at work, you'll want to do as good a job as possible – and you will!

• *Tuesday 20 August* •

You have your eyes set firmly on the future at the moment, yet it seems that other people can't tear themselves away from the past. As a result, you can expect some dramatic clashes today when you fail to see eye to eye. The more the other person wants to cling to the status quo or do things the traditional way, the more determined you will be to contradict them and stand up for what you believe in. And the battle isn't over yet!

• *Wednesday 21 August* •

The question of combining the old and the new, which was such a dominant factor yesterday, seems less problematic today. You can see ways round the current difficulties, so jot them down and make sure they're watertight. You will soon have to use these arguments when talking to others, and it's a good idea to make sure you've covered all the angles. You'll be pleased with what you come up with now, so put on your thinking cap.

• *Thursday 22 August* •

During the coming fortnight you'll become very embroiled in the current discussions about moving forward or abiding by the status quo. Tempers will be heated and nerves will be frayed, but it's important to stick to what you believe in. If you're involved in domestic improvements at the moment, be prepared to tidy up loose ends now. You may also have to stand your ground on certain questions.

• *Friday 23 August* •

Friends bring you some light relief from today and they'll be great company between now and late September. If your social life has fallen by the wayside recently because other commitments have taken up most of your time, this is a great chance to get back in the swing and catch up on all the gossip. A favourite hobby or pastime will also be good fun and help you to relax.

• *Saturday 24 August* •

It's perfectly obvious that someone won't take 'no' for an answer today, and they're being completely bloody-minded as a result. If you get involved in a discussion with them, it will quickly lead to an argument, with neither of you willing to back down. There may also be problems because someone wants to prove their independence and cut the apron strings, and that doesn't go down very well in some quarters. It may even lead to a massive scene. Tricky!

• *Sunday 25 August* •

If you've been meaning to sort out a nagging problem but simply haven't got around to it, give it a go today. Even if this is your day off, you'll feel better for having got this difficulty out of the way, and you'll be able to enjoy the rest of your Sunday with a clear conscience. If someone gets you involved in a discussion, you'll state your case in a way that leaves no room for doubt about what you think.

• *Monday 26 August* •

If you're wise, you'll keep your thoughts to yourself as much as possible over the next couple of months. That's partly because your ideas may be misconstrued or misused. It's also because you'll be reluctant to reveal too much of yourself, and will prefer to remain an enigma on certain subjects. However, make sure you speak up when it's important for you to voice an opinion. Otherwise someone may take your silence for assent or approval, even if you haven't given it.

• *Tuesday 27 August* •

This is a terrific day for making a big splash at work. You're determined to pull out all the stops and show where your talents lie. It's also great for beetling off to the gym or the sports ground and putting your body through its paces. Yes, you're feeling very energetic and lively, and you'll really enjoy doing things that are physical. They'll be very therapeutic.

• *Wednesday 28 August* •

It's so easy to get on well with other people today that you can't understand why it's sometimes like walking through a minefield. People are friendly, considerate and understanding now, and you're also in a very amenable mood. If you're considering ways to broaden your social life, this is a good day to start looking at what's available. How about joining a club or organization that appeals to you?

• *Thursday 29 August* •

You have renewed enthusiasm about adding to your stock of friends from today, and between now and mid-October you'll feel a strong urge to make the most of your social life. You'll also have a powerful yearning to forge ahead with your hopes and wishes for the future. If you don't seem to have got very far with your dreams this year, there's still plenty of 2002 left in which you can turn your hopes into reality.

• *Friday 30 August* •

There's an uncomfortable atmosphere today, especially when dealing with members of the family and partners. Everyone is feeling highly strung and ratty, and as a result it's one of those exhausting days when you all snap at each other and get thoroughly bad-tempered. It will be tempting to get drawn into petty squabbles and the sorts of argument where you go round in circles, especially if you feel you have to defend yourself.

• *Saturday 31 August* •

Oh dear! It's another day when tempers flare and everyone gets their knickers in a twist. This time, it looks as though the main problem is someone feeling that their freedom is being impinged upon or wanting to prove that they're completely independent even though they do it in a hurtful way. Be wary about mixing friends and finances because this will guarantee bad feeling and irritable explosions.

SEPTEMBER AT A GLANCE

Love	♥ ♥ ♥
Money	£ $
Career	💻 💻
Health	☼ ☼

• *Sunday 1 September* •

The past couple of days have been fractious to say the least, but things start to calm down again today. Phew! This is a big relief all round. It will also give you the chance to make amends and talk about what happened. There may be something that you want to apologize for. You certainly don't want to stand on ceremony, and if you have to eat a little humble pie in order to set the record straight then so be it.

• *Monday 2 September* •

You've got some great ideas today, especially when it comes to thinking about your long-term goals and objectives. It will help if you can mull things over by yourself because you're not yet keen to let others into your plans. If you're busy at work, you'll also get on best if you can be left to your own devices. It's not that you're feeling unfriendly, you'll simply function best on your own at the moment.

• *Tuesday 3 September* •

A loved one takes you by surprise today. They may drop in unannounced or ring you up, or they might tell you that they've arranged a special treat for you. If you've recently met someone and you're completely smitten by them, this is a perfect day to introduce them to selected members of the family. The atmosphere will be relaxed and there won't be any embarrassing questions or awkward silences.

• *Wednesday 4 September* •

You're in rather a nostalgic mood today and it won't take much to make your mind stray back down the years. You'll thoroughly enjoy a long wander down memory lane, especially if someone can share in your reminiscences. You might even be inspired to look through your photo albums, read your old diaries or leaf through some of your keepsakes. If you start to feel really sentimental, you may consider getting in touch with some of the people you haven't heard from in years. How about it?

• *Thursday 5 September* •

Any activities with a financial slant are time well spent now. You feel realistic about what you can achieve, and you're eager to sort out any problems that have been lingering on for too long. If you're toying with the idea of borrowing a large amount of money from a bank or building society, do your sums now while you're in the right mood. A partner will be cautious but they may have a point.

• *Friday 6 September* •

Get together with friends at some point today. They'll find you a real live wire and they'll really enjoy your company. If you've been considering joining a society or club and you're going along for the first time today to see what it's like, there's no need to feel nervous because you'll soon start chatting to other people. You may even bump into someone you know!

• *Saturday 7 September* •

A certain person is being very forceful today. They have a very clear idea of what they want to achieve, and they won't give up until they've got what they want. If you're the one who's feeling this way, try not to force your opinions on other people or coerce them into going along with your plans. This will work against you in the long run and may also make people suspicious or resentful of you, because they'll think you're being pushy.

• *Sunday 8 September* •

Take a look in the mirror over the next few weeks. What do you think of your reflection? If you're fed up with the face staring back at you, how can you liven up your image? Maybe a new hairdo is in order, or perhaps you're fed up with your current wardrobe? Don't feel that you have to spend a fortune – just a few minor adjustments may have a major impact on your appearance and ego. Have fun!

• *Monday 9 September* •

This is a good day to do some tidying up or turning out because you could find some things that you thought you'd lost for good. If you want to make room in your wardrobe and drawers for all the new clothes you're going to buy, and you're about to start throwing out things you'll never wear again, check the pockets first because you could find a few treasures nestling in there, such as money.

• *Tuesday 10 September* •

This is the perfect day to start altering your appearance in some way. If you haven't got a clue where to start, look through some magazines for ideas or talk to a friend and see what they suggest. You'll also enjoy browsing through your favourite shops or looking at some mail order catalogues. Don't feel you have to choose the same styles as usual – how about experimenting a little?

• *Wednesday 11 September* •

Something connected with your profession or home reaches a turning point today. For instance, your faith in a loved one may be restored after a period in which you doubted them, or you might finally make up your mind about some domestic issues. However, if you've been thinking the best of someone and turning a blind eye to their failings, the scales could come crashing from your eyes now, leaving you feeling massively disappointed in them.

• *Thursday 12 September* •

If you've been working hard recently, you'll receive a mini reward for all your efforts now. You might get a pat on the back or some words of praise, or you could be given a bonus or perk. There's even a chance that you might get a pay rise. Alternatively, if you think you deserve something but it isn't forthcoming, you may be tempted to drop a few hints and see what happens.

• *Friday 13 September* •

If you're the sort of Scorpio who can't help being superstitious, you'll soon start to blame the date when things go wrong today. But is that entirely fair? Perhaps the problem lies a little closer to home, and maybe it's because you're being difficult or obstinate? You may think that everyone else is being tricky while you're being all sweetness and light, but you might in fact be subconsciously provoking others into losing their temper with you. The situation isn't as cut and dried as it seems.

• *Saturday 14 September* •

Think twice before baring your soul and confiding in anyone between now and early October, because it could easily lead to you having egg smeared all over your face. For instance, you might realize when it's too late that you've given away more than you intended. There's even a chance that you could betray someone else's secret, even if you do it accidentally. You may also be on the receiving end of gossip about what you've told someone. If in doubt during the next few weeks, keep quiet.

• *Sunday 15 September* •

What's up with a certain person? They're all too eager to bite your head off, and they aren't very easy company at all. They may also be rather sarcastic or have a knack of saying things that get you on the raw. Unfortunately, you may also be infected by this bad mood, making you touchy and huffy. Try to work out what's really wrong and sort it out, rather than taking it out on whoever happens to be around.

• *Monday 16 September* •

In complete contrast to yesterday, everyone is in a sunny temper again today. It's a wonderful way to start the week because you're feeling optimistic and sociable. If you don't have anything nice lined up for the rest of the week, get on the phone and start making some arrangements. It would be a shame not to have anything to look forward to. Besides, friends will really enjoy having you around right now.

• *Tuesday 17 September* •

You're determined to see everything in a good light today, and you've no time for anyone who's feeling depressed or miserable. You'll soon tell them to buck their ideas up a bit! It's a super day to forge ahead with your long-term projects and goals, because you'll give them your best shot. You'll also get a big kick out of finding ways to improve your home or domestic set-up, even if you come up with rather modest ideas.

• *Wednesday 18 September* •

It feels like open house today! You could have a lot more visitors than usual, including one or two who you didn't expect to see. It's one of those days when you don't know what's going to happen next. Although this will be exciting at first, it could begin to pall after a while if it means you can't settle down to anything for long or you have to put your plans on hold because so many other things are happening instead. Yet it seems all you can do is to go with the flow.

• *Thursday 19 September* •

A loved one has their head in the clouds today. It's almost impossible to make them come down to earth, no matter how much you try. They refuse to look at the facts, especially if these are unpalatable or are in direct contravention of everything they like to think. This isn't a good day to make decisions about domestic improvements or a house sale because someone hasn't got their facts straight. You don't want to discover later on that you were stung or played for a fool.

• *Friday 20 September* •

A friend is full of energy today, and it will soon start to get on your nerves! They're bounding around like a two-year-old and they want to rope you into whatever they're doing. If you refuse to join in, they'll soon lose their temper with you. You may also start to feel rather impatient if you have to deal with someone who is dragging their heels or being a slowcoach. It will drive you to distraction.

• *Saturday 21 September* •

Today's Full Moon is highlighting the loving relationships in your life, and over the coming fortnight you may have to make important decisions connected with some of your favourite people. It will also be a marvellous chance to put the finishing touches to a project designed to showcase your artistic talents. You've worked hard at it and now is the time to bask in a blaze of compliments.

• *Sunday 22 September* •

Mind how you go today. You could easily lock horns with someone and end up at a complete stalemate with them. This is especially likely where finances are concerned, with neither of you willing to back down or acknowledge that the other person has a point. Instead, you'll both hold out to the bitter end, determined not to be the one who gives in first. It may appeal to your pride but it won't get you anywhere at all!

• *Monday 23 September* •

You've been very busy recently and you're starting to feel the need for some peace. Between now and late October is the perfect opportunity to tuck yourself away every now and then and revel in your own company. Think of it as your chance to recharge your batteries, both mentally and physically. It will do you the world of good to escape from life's hurly-burly once in a while and catch your breath.

• *Tuesday 24 September* •

This is a marvellous day to get on the right side of a boss or superior. They're in a very amenable mood, so make the most of it while it lasts! It's just what you need if you want to ask them a favour. If you're going to an office do or some sort of works outing, there could be a bit of a flirtation between you and someone in a position of power. Is it only harmless fun, or do you hope that something will come of it?

• *Wednesday 25 September* •

All your relationships go like clockwork today. People are being warm and affectionate, so everything goes well. There's only one tiny fly in the ointment, and that's someone who's feeling slightly jealous or envious. They may be rather defensive or they'll make it plain that they don't think life is fair. Try not to get into competition with this person because that will only make them feel worse.

• *Thursday 26 September* •

A certain person seems hell-bent on doing the opposite of whatever you tell them today. That's especially likely if it's a child or a close member of the family. They're being as stubborn as a mule and they're testing your patience to the limit. It's highly likely that there'll be a row before the day is over, because you'll find it almost impossible to contain your irritation and exasperation.

• *Friday 27 September* •

It's a strange day because you're feeling very communicative but you're not keen on being surrounded by lots of other people. Maybe the answer is to write things down, perhaps in your diary or in a journal. Or you might prefer to write someone a letter, telling them exactly how you feel. Treat secrets and confidences with great respect now otherwise someone may turn them into the latest gossip and then blame you for discussing them in the first place.

• *Saturday 28 September* •

If you're trying to organize a forthcoming social event, you'll wonder whether it's worth the effort today. Friends may raise lots of objections to your plans or someone might say they can't afford what you're suggesting. If you're going out on the town with some chums, make sure everyone has some idea of what it will cost so as to avoid embarrassing outbursts when the bill arrives.

• *Sunday 29 September* •

It's a day to mind your Ps and Qs, otherwise you're likely to put both feet in it. Be especially wary about getting drawn into conversations about religion, politics or any other social no-nos. They'll be a licence for red faces, heated disputes and people taking offence. This is the sort of day when you'll be wise to keep your opinions to yourself, even when you completely disagree with what you're being told.

• *Monday 30 September* •

The month ends on a high note, with you keen to enjoy yourself whenever you get the chance. It's a fabulous day for planning something that you can look forward to, particularly if it's connected with travel. For instance, if it seems like a long time since your last holiday or ages until your next vacation, how about planning a weekend away? You'll really enjoy having a change of scene.

OCTOBER AT A GLANCE

Love	♥ ♥ ♥ ♥ ♥
Money	£ $
Career	💻 💻
Health	☼ ☼ ☼ ☼ ☼

• *Tuesday 1 October* •

After the recent disturbances, peace breaks out again once more today. And long may it last! Grab this chance to make amends with any loved ones that you've fallen out with recently. You don't want the feud to last one minute longer than necessary, and today you're far more concerned about other people's hurt feelings than about your own. In fact, you're fully prepared to put your own needs on hold now and to concentrate on everyone else instead.

• *Wednesday 2 October* •

This is a day for working quietly by yourself, keeping your head down and not having a lot of contact with other people. That isn't because you're feeling unfriendly, simply because you'll enjoy having the space to think and the chance to be completely private. If you're working hard now, you'll do much better when left to yourself. A boss or superior will know they can trust you to get on with your work without them having to breathe down your neck.

• *Thursday 3 October* •

Life seems rather gloomy today. You're taking a very depressed outlook on life and will think the worst rather than take a more optimistic attitude. Although, as you keep reminding yourself, it's important to be realistic, do you have to be so doom-laden? It won't help if someone is making you feel bad or guilty, because that will just make you even more fed up than ever.

• *Friday 4 October* •

Your spirits rise again today and you're in the mood to get together with friends. It's time to let your hair down, especially if you've had rather a quiet week. Suddenly, you've emerged from your shell and you want to make contact with the rest of the world again. Even so, you aren't keen on anything very strenuous or noisy, so something like going out for a meal or a drink is perfect.

• *Saturday 5 October* •

You're still in a sociable mood, and today you're feeling more fiery than you were yesterday. You'll love the idea of doing something spontaneous, so you might grab you-know-who by the hand, scrap your usual Saturday routine and act on the spur of the moment. This is a great day for going to a party or gathering because you'll enjoy chatting to complete strangers. You'll probably come home with a string of phone numbers!

• *Sunday 6 October* •

If you've really enjoyed having some time to yourself lately, how about incorporating it into your daily routine in the future? Even if it means getting up before everyone else so you have the place to yourself, you'll relish the chance of privacy. Any form of relaxation technique is a good bet now, such as meditation or creative visualization. If you often get het up, you'll find it particularly useful now.

• *Monday 7 October* •

Life is full of excitement today, and the more the merrier as far as you're concerned. You'll welcome any little interruptions to your schedule as a chance to do something different for a change. If you're shopping for items for your home, don't be surprised if you're tempted by all sorts of unusual objects that would normally leave you cold. You can't resist the idea of some impulse buys now, but keep the receipts in case you change your mind tomorrow and want to take them back to the shop!

• *Tuesday 8 October* •

This is a fabulous day for getting to grips with your finances, especially if you've been putting things off recently or you're starting to worry about a big pile of bills facing you. If you're always forgetting to pay your bills or you sometimes have late payment charges on your credit cards, how about organizing yourself a little? Maybe you could set up some direct debit instructions or other ways of making things run smoothly without too much input from you?

• *Wednesday 9 October* •

Carry on the good work from yesterday and continue sorting out your finances. You're in a very sober frame of mind and you'll want to make sure you've dotted all the Is and crossed all the Ts. This is definitely not a day for leaving things to chance or overlooking some vital pieces of information. You're in a very responsible mood, but try to guard against a slight tendency to make a rod for your own back or do other people's jobs for them.

• *Thursday 10 October* •

There will be times during the next five weeks when it's difficult to be as demonstrative and affectionate as you would like. You'll feel a slight sense of reservation, as though something is holding you back, even if you're at a loss to explain what it is. You may also have doubts about your attractiveness and feel worried about what you see as flaws in your appearance. If you mention these to anyone else, they won't know what you're talking about!

• *Friday 11 October* •

Once again you feel a strong need to retreat into your shell today, and you won't be completely happy about emerging from it until later this month. In the meantime, use it as a chance to think things through. The year will soon be coming to a close, so how about thinking about all the things that have happened to you so far in 2002. Some of the events may take some getting used to, and it might help to talk things through with someone you can trust implicitly.

• *Saturday 12 October* •

The shops are calling! You're in the mood for some retail therapy, especially if that means kitting yourself out in some new clothes ready for the new season. Whatever you do today, you'll want to have fun at every opportunity and it won't take much to keep you happy. For instance, taking someone with you on your shopping trip and fitting in a meal at some point will be just what you're in the mood for.

• *Sunday 13 October* •

What's bugging you? You've got steam coming out of your ears. The trouble is that you will find it hard to express your anger, even if it's perfectly justified and it would be far better to say your piece than keep quiet. You may worry that if you lose your rag you'll say too much and end up feeling guilty, or perhaps you don't want to upset the person for some reason. Do your best to release your feelings in a positive and therapeutic way, otherwise you'll end the day in a right old state.

• *Monday 14 October* •

It feels as though you're beating your head against a brick wall today. You can't seem to make much progress and it doesn't help that certain people seem determined to stand in your way. There's not much you can do about this, especially at the moment, because you feel as though your hands are tied. It may be far better to switch to something else in which you feel you have more scope and are less dependent on other people's co-operation.

• *Tuesday 15 October* •

Between now and early December it won't always be easy to motivate yourself. There will be times when you feel as though nothing is going right and you're incapable of making the impact on others that you normally do. Even so, it will be important to push yourself forward whenever you think it's necessary, otherwise someone may take advantage of your reticence. You don't want to find that someone has made a fool out of you.

• *Wednesday 16 October* •

There's a lot happening today, especially at home. There are lots of comings and goings, and your normal Wednesday routine may be thrown out of whack completely by last-minute events. This suits your mood because you're feeling slightly restless and could easily become bored. If you're cooped up in one place for too long you'll certainly want to make a bid for freedom, and the more restrictive your circumstances the more determined you'll be to cut loose.

• *Thursday 17 October* •

If you want to get a boss or authority figure on your side, pull out all the stops today. Treat them like a human being rather than a faceless bureaucrat. It may also help to crack a few jokes! If you've been hoping that something romantic was going to happen with someone older or more powerful than you, there will be a slight disappointment today when things don't go as well as expected. But don't give up hope!

• *Friday 18 October* •

Give your imagination full rein today if you want to make the most of your brain. You're in a very creative mood and it will give you great pleasure to let your mind wander. Ignore anyone who talks disparagingly about daydreaming, or remind them that Einstein would never have discovered relativity if he hadn't been a daydreamer. However, it will be a struggle to concentrate on anything that's very detailed because you simply can't be bothered with it right now.

• *Saturday 19 October* •

Beware of being too hasty today because it will lead to upsets and might also cause a minor mishap. You'll soon be a complete butterfingers if you try to do things too quickly, so remember the story about the tortoise and the hare. Slow down! Be especially careful when handling anything hot or sharp because you could have a silly accident when you're distracted or you become all fingers and thumbs.

• *Sunday 20 October* •

Good news! You're in favour with the powers that be today. If you're at work, you'll receive a pat on the back from a boss. Even if you're at home, you may hear on the grapevine that you're in someone's good books at the moment. This is a very good day for thinking about your job prospects. You might find an advert for the perfect job in the papers or on the Internet, or someone may give you a useful tip-off.

• *Monday 21 October* •

The coming fortnight is the ideal time to take better care of your health. If you've been dragging yourself around like a wet lettuce recently or you're worried about an ailment that doesn't want to go away, start paying more attention to your well-being. Get some expert advice if you think it's necessary, and consider consulting a complementary practitioner if you haven't got anywhere with conventional medicine.

• *Tuesday 22 October* •

You're in a very serious-minded mood today and you aren't interested in any activities that you consider to be foolish or a waste of time. Instead, you want to tackle things that will improve your life in some way or which are long overdue. For example, it's a good day for getting to grips with your official finances or filling in complicated forms. You won't make any mistakes because you'll take such care first time round.

• *Wednesday 23 October* •

You start to emerge from your shell today! You're beginning to feel much more outgoing and sociable than you have recently, and you're keen to make up for lost time. The next four weeks will give you plenty of chances to do just that. You'll also be eager to get new plans off the ground, and you'll throw yourself into them with lots of determination and energy. As an added bonus, you'll enjoy a big surge in your popularity. Suddenly, it's all happening!

• *Thursday 24 October* •

You have a hankering for familiar faces and places today. You'll thoroughly enjoy surrounding yourself with loved ones, whether old or young. What's important to you now is to feel a sense of belonging with other people. If you're getting together with some of the family today you'll enjoy making it an extra nice time. If everyone is coming round to your place you may decide to push the boat out and cook something special.

• *Friday 25 October* •

Money threatens to come between you and certain people today. That's because it's an excuse to lose your temper with someone, or vice versa, especially if the real reason for the dispute seems too dangerous or taboo to mention. However, rather than have difficult topics acting like unexploded bombs, wouldn't it be better to sort them out now before they blow up in your face? It will be a weight off your mind.

• *Saturday 26 October* •

Yesterday's tensions have fled, leaving you feeling happy-go-lucky and keen to have as good a day as possible. Keep your eyes peeled for challenges because one might be right under your nose. Any activities connected with travel, education, politics or the environment go well now, and you may also get involved in a cause or crusade that's intended to make the world a better place. However, try not to convert everyone around you because they may want to make up their own minds.

• *Sunday 27 October* •

This is a fantastic day to think carefully about what you value in life. You shouldn't take anything for granted right now or assume that you'll have it for ever. So think about what and who makes your world go round, and whether you devote enough time to it. If you're currently trying to decide whether to make a major investment or a big change of direction, it's make-your-mind-up time. Suddenly, you're sure of your ground and you know exactly what your next step should be. Good luck!

• *Monday 28 October* •

You're very concerned about other people's welfare today, particularly if you can do something to improve it. You might get caught up in a good cause or voluntary group, or you may decide that charity begins at home and one of your relatives needs your help. You aren't interested in satisfying your own needs now – they come a very poor second to other people's desires and requirements, and you're pleased to do what you can to help.

• *Tuesday 29 October* •

What's wrong? It won't take much to put you on the defensive or imagine that everyone is out to get you. Perhaps someone is making snide remarks that have caught you on the raw? Or maybe you're rather annoyed that yesterday's self-sacrifice hasn't been appreciated in the way you would have liked. If that's the problem, you must ask yourself what you hoped to achieve by pandering to other people's needs. Were you looking for some brownie points?

• *Wednesday 30 October* •

Someone close to home isn't being realistic today. In fact, they seem to be living on another planet as far as you're concerned. Or is it the other way round? It will be very tempting to lose sight of reality now and to indulge in wishful thinking or even to block out unsavoury facts and hope that they go away. It's important that you come back down to earth of your own accord before life brings you down with a hefty bump.

• *Thursday 31 October* •

It may be Hallowe'en but you're all smiles today. The miserable mood of the past couple of days has evaporated, leaving you back on form. If you're going to a party to celebrate Hallowe'en, you'll enjoy making sure you look as good as possible. It might be the perfect excuse to buy a new outfit or visit the hairdresser. It's also a delicious day for your love life because a certain person thinks you're utterly irresistible at the moment, and you're not going to argue with them!

NOVEMBER AT A GLANCE

Love	♥ ♥ ♥ ♥ ♥
Money	£ $ £ $ £
Career	💻 💻 💻
Health	☼ ☼ ☼ ☼ ☼

• *Friday 1 November* •

Money worries put a crimp in your day. You're taking a rather gloomy view of your current finances, but are you justified in doing this? Perhaps things aren't nearly as awful as they seem? If a close partner or friend asks you for advice, your instincts will be to err on the side of caution or, as far as they're concerned, to be as pessimistic as possible. Come on, Scorpio, what's wrong?

• *Saturday 2 November* •

You're bursting to get something off your chest today but there are reasons why this isn't as simple as it seems. You may feel constrained by the circumstances or you might consider someone's feelings and not want to upset them. There is also a chance that you believe your own needs have to take a back seat at the moment, but this will soon make you feel very frustrated and hard done by.

• *Sunday 3 November* •

Life has a nice way of taking you by surprise today. It will certainly liven up the proceedings so there's no danger of you having a boring Sunday! If you're having an early party to celebrate Bonfire Night, things will go with a swing. However, it might be a good idea to lay in some extra food in case you have unexpected guests, or someone burns the sausages and you have to throw them away.

• *Monday 4 November* •

Today's New Moon will invigorate and energize you over the coming fortnight. It's a splendid chance to get a new venture off the ground or do anything else that will allow you to take the initiative. You certainly aren't content to rest on your laurels at the moment because there's so much you want to achieve. So if you've been waiting for the right time to start something new, that moment has now arrived.

• *Tuesday 5 November* •

An air of confusion makes this a difficult day, especially when it comes to making contact with your nearest and dearest. You may keep missing each other, which will be annoying and may even lead to a mix-up. The more you need someone to be straight with you, the more likely they are to fudge the issue or sound muddled. But before you point the finger of blame, bear in mind that you may also be muddying the waters or not being as straightforward as you imagine.

• *Wednesday 6 November* •

This is a fabulous day for buying items that will make your home more comfortable or cosy. You won't have to spend a fortune, either, so don't worry if you're trying to save money at the moment. Even a bunch of flowers will do the trick. If you're feeling more flush than that, consider altering some of your soft furnishings, such as changing the curtains or having the sofa reupholstered.

• *Thursday 7 November* •

There's good news on the money front today! It may not mean that you're about to receive a massive windfall so don't order that Rolls-Royce just yet. But you might find some cash lying on the pavement or discover some banknotes tucked away in one of your pockets. If you enjoy doing competitions and puzzles, give them a go now because you could be a winner. Even buying a raffle ticket might mean that you end up with a prize.

• *Friday 8 November* •

You're blessed with all the social graces today, so it's great for smoothing over any ruffled feathers or buttering someone up. It's a really good day for making contact with neighbours or close relatives, and you'll get on well together. If you're involved in a local enterprise or anything else that puts you in touch with the people in your neighbourhood, you'll hit it off with one person in particular and it might lead to an enjoyable friendship.

• *Saturday 9 November* •

You're in a very self-assured mood today, which is just what you need if you want to give a good impression or make a big impact on someone. However, you must try to stop short of sounding too big for your boots, because it's a fine line between confidence and cockiness. Alternatively, you'll have to deal with someone who thinks they're the bee's knees and who obviously expects you to agree with them. They'll give the impression that you should feel honoured to know them.

• *Sunday 10 November* •

You're fully prepared to stand your ground today over anything that you think is important, and you don't care what anyone else says on the subject. This will send out the message that you're in no mood to be trifled with, yet you'll manage to do this in a way that isn't threatening or arrogant. If you need to sort out a puzzle connected with your finances, get to the bottom of it now while you're in the mood.

• *Monday 11 November* •

Put on your thinking cap because you'll come up with some fabulous ideas today. You'll be especially inspired when it comes to thinking about your career, long-term goals and personal life. However, try not to over-reach yourself and get carried away, otherwise what started off as a fantastic scheme will become fantastical and impossible to put into action. Not even you will be able to pull it off, and that's saying something!

• *Tuesday 12 November* •

Loved ones help to put a spring in your step today. If possible, surround yourself with some of your favourite people at every opportunity because they'll make your life worth living. But there's no need to feel you're missing out if you can't be with those special people because you'll make a big effort to get on well with whoever happens to be around. They'll remember you as someone who's charming, sociable and amiable, and they'll probably want to see more of you in the future!

• *Wednesday 13 November* •

If you're at a loose end at some point today, do something that's enjoyable or which always makes you laugh. You're in a very relaxed and easy-going mood, and you're keen to make the most of it. You're also feeling generous so this is the perfect opportunity to start making your Christmas lists. Strolling around the shops or looking on the Internet will give you some good ideas about the gifts you can buy.

• *Thursday 14 November* •

You're so chatty today that you barely draw breath. In fact, it will be difficult for others to get a word in edgeways! Although you're full of things you want to talk about, try to consider other people's feelings and let them have their fair share of the conversation. You're in a very subjective mood now, so it will be difficult to think about anything rationally or dispassionately. It's simply not the way your mind is working at the moment.

• *Friday 15 November* •

If someone isn't feeling very well, they're getting elderly or there are other reasons why they're struggling at the moment, you'll want to help them in any way you can. You might do their shopping for them, run some errands for them or stay and keep them company. While you're so concerned about other people's welfare, make sure your nearest and dearest are OK as well. Be aware that someone may need your help but feel shy about asking for it.

• *Saturday 16 November* •

You have a lot on your mind today and it's difficult to know where to start. As a result, you will feel that you should be doing about five things at once and you may be tempted to cut corners to save time. This is a tricky day because you'll struggle to concentrate on anything for long. Your mind will keep straying off the subject and it won't help that you're feeling so restless and fidgety. Avoid making important domestic plans because you may leap into things without thinking them through.

• *Sunday 17 November* •

Once again you're feeling restless and edgy. If you know exactly what's wrong, try to do something about it before you drive yourself to distraction. However, it's far more likely that you don't have a clue why you've got ants in your pants at the moment. Sitting around will soon have you at screaming pitch, so go for a brisk walk, turn out some cupboards, or do anything else that will help you to burn up all that excess nervous energy.

• *Monday 18 November* •

Someone's in rather a distracted mood today and it will be difficult to shake them out of it. In fact, it will probably be far better to leave them alone for the time being and try again another day when they're more on the ball. However, it may not be that simple. For instance, you may suspect that this person is holding out on you and deliberately being vague. Perhaps they've transgressed in some way and they want to throw you off the scent? Or are you being paranoid? What a day!

• *Tuesday 19 November* •

Between now and early December is a marvellous chance to consider where you stand financially. Look at all your options and be prepared to make some decisions that will improve your current circumstances. If necessary, talk to a financial expert or anyone else who knows how to make their money grow. It will also be a good opportunity to buy items that will improve your communications in some way, such as a new computer or a mobile phone.

• *Wednesday 20 November* •

The coming couple of weeks will be a very important phase in your one-to-one relationships. They may even signal that it's make-or-break time where a certain person is concerned. If there have been problems with someone recently, matters are about to come to head, forcing you to take decisive action. This won't be easy but you'll realize that you don't have much choice and that it's essential to show exactly where you stand. If you handle it well, there won't have to be a showdown.

• *Thursday 21 November* •

At times over the past few weeks you've felt as though you were slightly separated from everyone around you. It may have been hard to make emotional contact with them and you might even have been aware of a vague rift between you. But that starts to disappear from today, leaving you feeling much more emotionally forthcoming and friendly. If you inadvertently hurt someone during this phase, start to make amends now.

• *Friday 22 November* •

During the next four weeks you'll gain a lot of insight from thinking about everything that you value in life. If your priorities always seem to have to take a back seat to your work or your relationships, start to consider how you can change the balance a little. This doesn't have to be a licence to be completely selfish but it is a chance to introduce more meaning into your life or allocate a few minutes each day when you do something that puts a huge smile on your face.

• *Saturday 23 November* •

If you've been smarting recently because a certain person seems to think that you're their property, they always take you for granted, or they treat you as though you're about four years old, this is a good day to raise a modest flag of revolution. You won't have to make a big song and dance to get your point across, and even dropping the odd hint might do the trick. Provided they feel they're still part of your life, they won't mind allowing you a little more freedom.

• *Sunday 24 November* •

You're in a very imaginative mood today, particularly when it comes to thinking about your home and family. Trust your intuition because it will guide you in the right direction. If someone wants to pour their heart out to you, you'll instinctively know the right things to say to make them feel better. And if the boot's on the other foot and you need a shoulder to cry on, talk to someone who knows you inside out.

• *Monday 25 November* •

Concentrate on your long-term plans and goals today. You're eager to bring them one step closer to reality, even if the final outcome is still a long way off. If you need to find ways to finance these ambitions, put on your thinking cap or talk to someone who may be able to help. Keeping a positive attitude is the first step to success now so don't write off your aspirations simply because they'll involve a lot of effort on your part. Don't be faint-hearted!

• *Tuesday 26 November* •

Carry on the good work from yesterday and continue to focus on your long-distance plans. But don't neglect your current job and responsibilities because you can get a lot done now. This is a super day for chatting to a boss or authority figure because you'll soon be able to get on the right side of them. If you have some suggestions to make, get them off your chest now while they're guaranteed a favourable reception.

• *Wednesday 27 November* •

There's a tremendous amount to achieve today, but you may do most of it behind the scenes or on the QT. This certainly isn't a day for doing things in the limelight if you can possibly avoid it – you'll feel so much more comfortable when working behind the scenes. If you're someone's right-hand man or woman, you'll be thrilled with what happens now and you'll be reminded that you're doing a really good job.

• *Thursday 28 November* •

Be careful when sorting out anything financial today as tempers will soon become frayed. You will also struggle to remain objective. Ideally, you should keep money and chums as far apart as possible because they're a recipe for disaster right now. Someone may raise petty objections that make your hackles rise, or there could be a nit-picking argument over ridiculous details. Not an easy day!

• *Friday 29 November* •

If you got fed up with going round in circles yesterday, do your best to straighten out the situation today. Everyone has calmed down and things won't be nearly as fraught, even if you're talking about difficult topics. If you're meeting up with a friend or a very special someone, the conversation will soon stray to subjects that are dear to your heart. You'll have a very enjoyable time!

• *Saturday 30 November* •

If you're a typical Scorpio you're blessed with X-ray vision and this is the ideal day to focus on your finances. If there's a problem, you'll soon spot it because there are no flies on you at the moment. In fact, anyone who tries to pull the wool over your eyes now will soon regret it. You have remarkable powers of concentration today but do your best not to get bogged down in detail or to become obsessed with something to such an extent that you can't think about anything else.

DECEMBER AT A GLANCE

Love	♥ ♥ ♥
Money	£ $ £ $ £
Career	💻 💻
Health	☼ ☼ ☼

• *Sunday 1 December* •

Home comforts make you feel good today. In fact, you won't want to stray too far from your own front door if you can possibly avoid it. Your idea of heaven now is to have some of your nearest and dearest around you and to make a great big fuss of them. If you're doing the cooking today you'll enjoy pulling out all the stops, perhaps by preparing someone's favourite meal or starting the festive preparations. If you haven't yet made the Christmas cake you might feel inspired to start any minute now!

• *Monday 2 December* •

Expect to feel a surge of energy today that will carry you through the rest of the month with aplomb and dynamism. If you were starting to get fed up with sitting back while everyone else occupied the limelight, you're now ready to make a big splash again. It's just what you need if you're looking forward to a socially hectic December. You'll manage to go to lots of parties without flagging, and you'll still have the energy to get new projects off the ground. It's going to be quite a month!

• *Tuesday 3 December* •

If you find yourself gritting your teeth today, it's a sign that events are starting to get to you. This is one of those irritating days when nothing goes quite according to plan, and you may end up chasing your tail or having to deal with time-wasters. There won't be much you can do about this, either, so your best bet is to grin and bear it. At least it won't last long.

• *Wednesday 4 December* •

If December is always an expensive month for you, try to work out a budget sooner rather than later. Today's Totally Eclipsed New Moon signals the start of a fresh phase in your financial life, when you're ready to turn over a new leaf, learn from previous mistakes and enter 2003 feeling confident about your monetary status. This is a fabulous time to make a major investment or purchase, provided you've got your sums right and you know you're using your money wisely.

• *Thursday 5 December* •

Someone close to home has some wacky ideas today but they're definitely worth listening to. Even if you think this person is talking nonsense at first, you'll soon realize there's method in their madness and they're seeing things from a very innovative point of view. You're also in an inventive frame of mind now, particularly when thinking about your domestic life.

• *Friday 6 December* •

If possible, avoid talking about money today because the conversation will soon start to depress you. People are being very cautious and possibly even pessimistic, and if you ask their advice about something financial you'll soon wish you hadn't because what they say will have your heart crashing down to your boots. If a bill arrives today it will make you feel wretched, but try not to over-react – it isn't the end of the world.

• *Saturday 7 December* •

Ideally, you should spend today going over existing plans and making sure they're on the right track. If you try to launch something new now you might find that it's a complete waste of time and that nothing comes of it. Your social life could suffer from petty irritations, such as someone not turning up on time. Short journeys will be affected too, so be prepared for delays, misinformation or traffic jams.

• *Sunday 8 December* •

Your mind starts buzzing today and you'll be in a very inquisitive mood throughout the rest of December. It's the perfect opportunity to meet up with friends and catch up on all the gossip. You'll also enjoy doing lots of reading and writing, so it's the ideal time to get your Christmas cards out of the way long before the last posting dates. The only snag is that your phone bill may be larger than usual because you'll be unable to resist ringing up all sorts of people.

• *Monday 9 December* •

Your finances have been a major theme in your life over the past few weeks and by now you should have a pretty good idea of how to make improvements or adjustments to your current monetary situation. Any action that you take today stands a good chance of being a success because you won't waste your time on anything that seems silly or inconsequential. You may even make decisions in a very resolute way because the situation seems so clear to you at the moment. You will have no doubts that you're doing the right thing.

• *Tuesday 10 December* •

You're buoyed up by a strong sense of optimism today. You know you're doing well and you have good reason to feel pleased with yourself. If one of your projects at the moment is to look for a job with better prospects, keep a sharp look out today because you might spot something that's right up your street. It's also a good day for making contact with people in power because they're looking at you very favourably at the moment.

• *Wednesday 11 December* •

Any hint of possessiveness or jealousy won't go down at all well today. It may even provoke the sort of fireworks that wouldn't have been out of place on Bonfire Night. If this is something that's been simmering in the background for ages, do your best to clear the air now. It won't help to ignore the situation because that will only lead to further resentment. You need to thrash things out so everyone knows where they stand.

• *Thursday 12 December* •

Money causes plenty of ructions today, especially when other people get involved in the equation. For instance, if you're out shopping with a loved one you might have a row about what to buy, or there could be a difference of opinion about how much to spend on someone's Christmas present. One of you is being rather mean and miserly, and the other one objects strongly.

• *Friday 13 December* •

The past couple of days haven't exactly been a bed of roses so it's a great relief to know that, despite the date, today's much more relaxed and enjoyable. Grab any chance to unwind after the recent flak because it will do you lots of good. If you were going out on the town you may even decide to postpone it until you're more in the mood, and instead luxuriate at home. Maybe you could put up some festive decorations and then sit and admire them?

• *Saturday 14 December* •

A certain someone is very reluctant to face up to the truth today, and it's a waste of time trying to make them change their mind. Who is this person? Well, actually, it might be you! There's a distinct possibility that you're wearing rose-tinted glasses and you refuse to take them off. Be very wary if you're currently involved in a house purchase or home improvement plan because you may be ignoring warning signs that things aren't going as well as expected.

• *Sunday 15 December* •

There's nothing you'll like better today than a cosy chat with someone. You'll thoroughly enjoy sharing all the latest news with them. Any activities that bring you into contact with your neighbours are good fun now, so if you don't have anything planned how about inviting someone in for a drink? You have a keen eye for beauty today and you'll love taking a walk in some attractive surroundings.

• *Monday 16 December* •

This is a marvellous day to think about making changes to your domestic life and how you're going to finance them. You're in the happy position of being able to blend caution with enterprise and tradition with innovation, so you'll have the best of both worlds. Ideally, you should involve other people in what you're planning, not only because it may affect them but also because you'll benefit from their input and advice.

• *Tuesday 17 December* •

How are your festive preparations coming along? This is an excellent day to check that everything is going smoothly and that you haven't overlooked anything vital. It's a good idea to plan for last-minute emergencies and unexpected developments, so how about buying some extra gifts just in case you need them? Speaking of which, a loved one may have a little surprise for you that certainly brightens up your day.

• *Wednesday 18 December* •

Any decisions that you take today stand an excellent chance of being a success, particularly where your finances and your long-term prospects are concerned. What's more, they may have a profound impact on your life over the next few months, so don't take these decisions lightly. It's an ideal opportunity to start making your New Year resolutions while you're in such a far-sighted and positive mood. Don't underestimate yourself – you're capable of great things.

• *Thursday 19 December* •

During the coming fortnight you need to turn your attention to your close and intimate relationships. If you suspect that you've been neglecting your other half recently because you've had so much on your plate, now is your chance to make it up to them. Remind them how important they are to you and be prepared to discuss your feelings with them. This is no time to maintain an enigmatic silence – let them into your confidence, even if that means talking about subjects that are usually off limits.

• *Friday 20 December* •

Life has plenty to offer today and you're eager to get as much excitement out of the day as possible. You're in a very adventurous mood and you'll jump at the chance to do something out of the ordinary or which you've never tried before. After all, there's a first time for everything! Travel appeals to you now and you may be toying with the idea of going far afield on your next holiday.

• *Saturday 21 December* •

You've very quick to jump to conclusions today and you'll pride yourself on being so decisive and objective. But actually you may be ignoring the salient facts and basing your ideas on nothing more than hunches and gut instincts. Be very careful when discussing such subjects as politics, religion or the environment because you could soon become embroiled in a hot-headed discussion that could lead to a bad-tempered dispute.

• *Sunday 22 December* •

You'll have a strong desire to communicate with people over the next four weeks. As a result, you'll thoroughly enjoy chattering to whoever happens to be around. It will be very important for you to get your ideas across and if you can't have your say you'll feel stymied and frustrated. The trick will be to voice your opinions without dominating conversations or sounding as though you're giving a lecture. If you see someone's eyes glazing over you'll know what's happening!

• *Monday 23 December* •

If you're trying to hit a deadline before the Christmas holidays begin, you'll feel as though you're running round in circles today. Rather than waste time and energy on getting into a panic about all the things you still have to do, focus on one task at a time. If you try to take on too much at once you'll only get into a state and slow yourself down. Channelling your energy in the right direction will be very productive.

• *Tuesday 24 December* •

You're starting to feel very festive! In fact, as far as you're concerned, the holidays start here! You're all set to open a bottle of wine and begin celebrating, preferably in the company of friends, neighbours and relatives. If you're going to a social event you'll be the life and soul of the party. You will also find it surprisingly easy to chat away to complete strangers, even if you're often tongue-tied when meeting new people.

• *Wednesday 25 December* •

Happy Christmas! You're all set for a whale of a time because you're in a wonderfully festive mood. What's more, you want everyone else to enjoy themselves and you'll bend over backwards to make sure it happens. Don't worry about keeping older relatives amused or trying to get on the right side of an awkward customer because things will go much better than expected. Someone older or more influential than you may make you a promise, so listen carefully. But whether they keep it is another matter!

• *Thursday 26 December* •

What's wrong? Someone isn't nearly as chirpy as they were yesterday. In fact, they're being downright morose and lousy company. They may even be displaying killjoy tendencies that put a dampener on the festivities. If you're the one with a long face, try to do something therapeutic rather than mope around and make yourself even more miserable. If you're worried about something, remind yourself that it may not be nearly as awful as you think.

• *Friday 27 December* •

A certain person appears to have lost their sense of humour. They're disgruntled and seem to be spoiling for a fight. It's a day when hidden tensions come to the surface, demanding to be released. Someone is full of recriminations or accusations, and you'll get the distinct impression that they've been brooding over them for some time now. It's no use glossing over them – you need to clear the air, and fast.

• *Saturday 28 December* •

The recent difficulties have left you feeling agitated and restless, but you don't have to stay that way. Seize the chance to do something energetic today, whether that means cleaning the car until you can see your reflection in the paintwork or working off your frustrations in the gym. Once you've calmed down you'll be ready to turn your attention to your goals and ambitions, and think about what you want to achieve in 2003.

• *Sunday 29 December* •

Peace breaks out today after the recent hostilities and you're eager to kiss and make up. Once you've got the apologies out of the way you can start to enjoy yourself again. You're feeling sociable, so how about visiting someone you didn't see during the festivities? Or maybe you'd prefer to go out for a meal, especially if you're getting fed up with leftover turkey? If you're back at work tomorrow it's even more important to have some fun today.

• *Monday 30 December* •

Adrenalin surges through you today, making you feel powerful and as though you can do almost anything. It's just what you need if you want to put yourself in the limelight or attract someone's attention. You're also operating at a much faster pace than normal. However, there's a chance that you could become rather hot-tempered if things don't go the way you want. You will also soon get frustrated when dealing with anyone who wants to take things nice and slowly.

• *Tuesday 31 December* •

You're in the mood to unwind and relax today. If you're still on holiday, you'll take great pleasure in doing as little as possible. You may even think twice about getting out of bed! If you're at work, you'll feel happiest when involved in creative and artistic tasks that allow you to daydream. When it comes to seeing in the New Year, you'll feel most comfortable if you're surrounded by familiar faces. Have a good time!

YOUR SCORPIO SUN SIGN

In this chapter I am going to tell you all about your Scorpio Sun sign. But what is a Sun sign? It often gets called a star sign, but are they the same thing? Well, yes, although 'Sun sign' is a more accurate term. Your Sun sign is the sign that the Sun occupied when you were born. Every year, the Sun moves through the heavens and spends an average of 30 days in each of the twelve signs. When you were born, the Sun was moving through the sign of Scorpio, so this is your Sun or star sign.

This chapter tells you everything you want to know about your Sun sign. To start off, I describe your general personality – what makes you tick. Then I talk about your attitude to relationships, the way you handle money, what your Sun sign says about your health and, finally, which careers are best for you. Put all that together and you will have a well-rounded picture of yourself.

Character

Intense and passionate about life, you never like to do things by halves. You believe that if something is worth doing, it's worth doing properly. You apply this logic to every aspect of your life, from shopping to sex. It's this intensity that makes you so mysterious to the rest of us. There's a lot more going on inside you than you're prepared to admit, because you're very private and you like to keep things to yourself. Your Water element means you're extremely sensitive to situations and people, but you're especially interested in fathoming out what's going on under the surface. If there's a rat around, you'll usually be able to sniff it out!

You are ruled by Pluto, the planet of transformation, and it shows. The lives of many Scorpios are divided up into distinct chapters – you have the knack of making a clean break and moving on to something new with barely a backward glance.

It's essential for you to have power and control over your life. You loathe the very idea of being at someone else's mercy or whims, and need to know that you're in the driving seat. This can sometimes make you seem rather formidable to everyone around you, because you will control situations and people without realizing it.

Most of your emotions are going on under the surface, and it can be difficult for you to be open about how you're feeling. Anger and resentment can seethe away beneath an apparently calm exterior until you reach breaking point and all hell is let loose!

Relationships

As with every other area of your life, you take your relationships very seriously. You put your heart and soul into them, because otherwise you can't really see the point in having them. Partners and friends will be left in no doubt about their importance in your life. You may even tell them that you were fated to know each other.

Your need for control can make you a pretty powerful partner. If you've been badly hurt in the past, you may be reluctant to let your partner out of your sight for long, in case they get up to something that you'll find threatening. Many Scorpios ruin perfectly good relationships by being too controlling, possessive and jealous, which makes them even more determined to exert an iron grip on their future partners. The whole thing ends up being a vicious circle.

Your immense loyalty and fidelity mean you will support loved ones through thick and thin. If they're in trouble, you'll do what you can to help them. You also tend to keep your friends for years, staying in touch with people you met at school or college for the rest of your life. You can't see any reason not to. However, if anyone hurts you badly or does something that you think is unforgivable, you may cut them out of your life completely in case they do it again. Once bitten, twice shy!

Money

This is a subject that you understand and respect! You like money because it enables you to stay in control of things. You don't like the thought of being dependent on others, or the state, to pay the bills. If you share a joint account with someone, you probably try to control the purse strings. You may tell yourself that your partner is too busy to do it or is not financially minded, even though those aren't the real reasons for you wanting to be in charge!

When you have money to spare, you don't like frittering it away. You aren't the sort of person to spend money just for the sake of it, and even if you're very well off you may be reluctant to part with it. Some Scorpios enjoy buying status symbols such as expensive cars or big houses because these make a big statement to the world that the Scorpio is doing OK for themselves. Occasionally, however, these can eventually become a burden because the Scorpio has to work hard to maintain their lavish lifestyle.

Your careful approach to finance means you enjoy tracking down the best rate of interest available at any one time and researching to see which credit card offers the best deal. There's no way anyone can fob you off with unfounded sales talk. You'll spot them coming a mile off!

Health

The intensity with which you approach life doesn't always do your health a lot of favours. If you tend to bottle up your feelings, it can have adverse effects on your blood pressure and digestive system. Scorpio rules the bowels and sexual organs, and many Scorpios can suffer from problems in these areas. You may also have throat problems every now and then.

You have a lot of stamina and endurance, but even so you should take care of yourself. Try not to work yourself into the ground too often because it won't do you any good. You may be able to work round the clock when you're under a lot of pressure but you shouldn't do this regularly. Instead, you need plenty of time to yourself – Scorpio is quite a solitary sign and you enjoy your privacy. If you're constantly surrounded by other people and can only be alone in the bathroom, it will soon start to get to you.

Because you belong to the Water element, any relaxation that involves water is good for you. You might enjoy swimming or maybe you fancy something more exciting and dangerous, such as water-skiing, jet-skiing, scuba diving or white-water rafting. There's nothing namby-pamby about you! (After all, this is the sign of James Bond!) When you need some quiet time to yourself, you might gain a lot of emotional satisfaction from strolling by an ocean or lake.

Career

Whatever you do for a living, it has to give you pleasure and satisfaction. If your job is mindless or you always count the hours until it's time to leave, you'll soon start to feel frustrated and as though you're wasting your life.

Ideally you need a career that offers plenty of emotional depth and gives you something to get your teeth into. Many Scorpios are fascinated by psychology, psychotherapy and psychiatry, because they enjoy unravelling people's complex personalities. Hypnotism is another very Scorpio technique. Other suitable professions for you are finance, medicine, science (especially geology and vulcanology) and the funeral business.

If you're working in an office with other people, you won't want to be the minion. Even if you have to start at the bottom, you won't want to stay on that lowly rung of the ladder for long! Sometimes this can make you seem very ambitious, and your boss may even wonder if you've got your eye on their job! (They're probably right!) You enjoy getting involved in all the office intrigue that's going on, and are probably one of the first to know the latest gossip. Your tremendous sensitivity may mean you're a shoulder to cry on when colleagues are having a bad time. When times are good, you'll happily take part in work expeditions to the local pub or wine bar. No wonder you're a very popular member of the team!

LOVE AND THE STARS

Have you ever wondered why you get on so well with some signs and never seem to hit it off with others? Do you send out stacks of birthday cards at particular times of the year because you know so many people born under those signs, while you don't know anyone who's born at other times of the year? Have you ever wondered why this is? Well, astrology has the answers!

If you're fed up with your relationships being like a lottery, because you aren't sure if you'll hit the jackpot or end up with nothing, this guide will give you some astrological help in getting on well with the people around you. It's arranged sign by sign, with your own sign heading the list. I describe how you get on with each sign – what brings you together or perhaps what can drive you apart. Once you've read about how your sign gets on with the other members of the zodiac, you can read what the other signs think of you! Turn to the sign of your friend or your partner and find out how they get along with you. You might gain some very interesting insights into how your relationship works. Do you get on like a house on fire, or is it more like fireworks when you get together?

At the end of my astrological guide to love, there are two compatibility charts so you can see at a glance how you get on with all the Sun signs, as lovers and also as friends. Each combination has been marked out of ten, so you can see whether you're soulmates or your relationship requires lots of work. Ten means it's everything you ever wanted while one means that you feel like asking for your money back. Having said that, don't panic if your current relationship gets a low score. Every Sun sign combination has the potential to be a success, but some are easier to deal with than others.

All you need to do is look for the woman's Sun sign along the top of the chart and then find the man's sign down the side. The box where the two meet will show how well they get on together.

Scorpio

Not every sign gets on well with its fellow members, yet an astonishing number of Scorpios pair up. They feel safe together because they know the worst and best about each other. When things are good, they're brilliant but these two can also bring out the worst in each other, with intense silences and brooding sulks. A Scorpio enjoys the tender ministrations of a loving Cancerian, and adores being with someone who's so obviously concerned about their welfare. Feelings run deep when a Scorpio pairs up with a Piscean, although the Scorpio may become impatient with the Piscean's reluctance to face up to unpalatable truths.

The three Earth signs – Taurus, Virgo and Capricorn – are well suited to the Scorpio temperament. Those astrological opposites, Scorpio and Taurus, enjoy a powerful relationship, much of which probably takes place in the bedroom, but whenever they have a disagreement there's an atmosphere you could cut with a knife, and neither of them will be prepared to admit they were in the wrong. A Scorpio is attracted to a neat, analytical Virgo but their feelings will be hurt by this sign's tendency to criticize.

What's more, their pride stops them telling the Virgo how they feel. The Scorpio admires a practical Capricorn, especially if they've earned a lot of respect through their work, but this could be a rather chilly pairing because both signs find it difficult to show their feelings.

When you put a Scorpio together with one of the three Fire signs, they'll either get on famously or won't understand one another at all. A Scorpio revels in the lusty Arien's sex drive, although they'll soon feel tired if they try to keep up with the Arien's busy schedule. The combination of Scorpio and Leo packs quite a punch. They're both very strong personalities, but they boss one another around like mad and find it almost impossible to achieve a compromise if they fall out. A Scorpio likes to take life at a measured pace, so they're bemused by a Sagittarian's need to keep busy all the time. In the end, they'll become fed up with never seeing the Sagittarian, or playing second fiddle to all their other interests.

Scorpio is bemused by the three Air signs – Gemini, Libra and Aquarius – because they operate on such completely different wavelengths. A Scorpio can be good friends with a Gemini but they're at emotional cross-purposes, with the Scorpio's intense approach to life too much for a light-hearted Gemini to cope with. Emotions are also the bugbear between a Scorpio and a Libran. Everything is great at first, but the Scorpio's powerful feelings and dark moods will eventually send the Libran running in the opposite direction. You can expect some tense arguments when a Scorpio pairs up with an Aquarian – they're both convinced that they're right and the other one is wrong.

Sagittarius

When a Sagittarian pairs up with a fellow Fire sign, there's plenty of warmth and the odd firework. A Sagittarian is thrilled by the adventurous spirit of an Arien, and they love exploring the world together. There are plenty of tall tales when a Sagittarian gets together with a Leo – they'll try to outdo each other, dropping names and recounting their greatest triumphs. If the Leo is slightly pompous, the Sagittarian is able to take them down a peg or two, but they must beware of hurting the Leo's feelings. As for two Sagittarians, they'll spur each other on and encourage one another to gain as much experience of life as possible. You probably won't be able to move in their house for books.

With their endless curiosity about the world, Sagittarians understand the intellectual Air signs very well. A Sagittarian enjoys the chatty company of a Gemini and, because they're opposite numbers in the zodiac, the Sagittarian is able to encourage the Gemini to see things through and explore them in more detail than usual. A refined and diplomatic Libran will try to teach the blunt Sagittarian not to say the first thing that pops into their head. However, the Sagittarian may eventually find the Libran's sense of balance rather trying – why can't they get more worked up about things? There's plenty of straight talking when a Sagittarian teams up with an Aquarian – they both have a high regard for honesty. The independent Sagittarian respects the Aquarian's need for freedom, but may feel rather stung by their periods of emotional coolness.

A Sagittarian will struggle to understand the Earth signs. They respect the Taurean's ability to work hard but they're driven to distraction by their reluctance to make changes and break out of any ruts they've fallen into. A Sagittarian enjoys talking to a brainy Virgo, but their expansive and spontaneous nature could eventually be restricted by the Virgo's need to think things through before taking action. When a Sagittarian gets together with a Capricorn, it's a case of optimism versus pessimism. While the Sagittarian's glass is half-full, the Capricorn's is always half-empty, and this causes many rows and possibly some ill feeling.

There could be lots of misunderstandings when a Sagittarian gets involved with one of the Water signs. A Sagittarian needs a bigger social circle than their family, whereas a Cancerian is quite happy surrounded by kith and kin. The Sagittarian need for independence won't go down well, either. It's like oil and water when a Sagittarian pairs up with a Scorpio. The Sagittarian is the roamer of the zodiac, whereas the Scorpio wants them where they can see them, in case they're up to no good. All will be well if the Sagittarian gets together with a strong-minded Piscean. In fact, they'll really enjoy one another's company. A Piscean who's lost in a world of their own, however, will soon leave them cold.

Capricorn

Despite their outward poise, a Capricorn is very easily hurt so they need to know their feelings won't be trampled on. There's least danger of that when they get together with a fellow Earth sign. A Capricorn adores a Taurean's deep sense of responsibility and they'll both work hard to create their ideal home. A Capricorn appreciates the methodical approach of a Virgo, but could feel deeply hurt by the Virgo's sharp tongue and caustic remarks. If two Capricorns team up, one of them must be demonstrative and openly affectionate, otherwise the relationship could be rather sterile and serious.

Capricorns also feel safe with members of the Water signs. When a Capricorn gets together with a Cancerian, they do their utmost to make their home a haven. They'll get great satisfaction from channelling their energies into bringing up a family. A Capricorn may be rather bemused by the depth and intensity of a Scorpio's emotions – Capricorns are too reserved to indulge in such drama themselves and it can make them feel uncomfortable. A no-nonsense Capricorn could be perplexed by an extremely vulnerable Piscean and won't know how to handle them. Should they give them a hanky or tell them to pull themselves together?

The Air signs can also make a Capricorn feel somewhat unsettled. They're fascinated by a Gemini's breadth of knowledge and endless chat, but they also find them superficial and rather flighty. In fact, the Capricorn probably doesn't trust the Gemini. A Capricorn feels far happier in the company of a Libran. Here's someone who seems much steadier emotionally and who can help the Capricorn to unwind after a hard day's work. It can be great or ghastly when a Capricorn sets their sights on an Aquarian. They understand each other provided the Aquarian isn't too unconventional, but the Capricorn feels uncomfortable and embarrassed by any displays of eccentricity, deliberate or not.

The Fire signs help to warm up the Capricorn, who can be rather remote and distant at times. A Capricorn admires the Arien's drive and initiative, but endlessly tells them to look before they leap and could become irritated when they don't take this sage advice. When a Capricorn gets together with a Leo, they won't need to worry about appearances – the Capricorn will feel justly proud of the smart Leo. However, they could wince when the bills come in and they discover how much those clothes cost. A Capricorn thinks a Sagittarian must have come from another planet – how can they be so relaxed and laid-back all the time? They have great respect for the Sagittarian's wisdom and philosophy, but they quickly become fed up with having to fit in around the Sagittarian's hectic social life.

Aquarius

Put an Aquarian with a fellow Air sign and they're happy. They thoroughly enjoy being with a lively Gemini and love discussing everything under the sun with them. They may not have a very exciting sex life, but their mental closeness will more than make up for it. The gentle charm of a Libran calms down an Aquarian when their nerves become frayed, although they disapprove of the Libran's innate tact and diplomacy – why can't they just say what they think, instead of sitting on the fence? With two Aquarians you never know what to expect, other than that they'll be great friends. They'll certainly do a lot of talking, but could spend more time debating esoteric ideas and abstract concepts.

An Aquarian likes all the Fire signs, although they find Ariens hard to fathom and can become exhausted by an Arien's endless supply of energy and enthusiasm. There are no such problems when an Aquarian pairs up with a Leo because they complement each other in many ways. The Aquarian teaches objectivity to the Leo, who in return encourages the Aquarian to express their emotions more. An Aquarian thoroughly enjoys being with a Sagittarian because both of them hate being tied down. As a result, they respect one another's independence and will probably rarely see each other because of all their spare-time activities.

It's not quite so simple when an Aquarian joins forces with one of the Earth signs. An Aquarian will lock horns with a Taurean sooner or later, because neither of them is able to back down once a disagreement has started. The Aquarian will also feel very restricted by the Taurean's possessiveness. The Virgo's analytical approach to life intrigues the Aquarian but they'll sit up all night arguing the toss over everything, with each one convinced that they've got all the answers. When an Aquarian meets a Capricorn, they've got their work cut out for them if they're to find a happy medium between the erratic Aquarian and the conventional Capricorn.

An Aquarian feels out of their depth when they're with one of the Water signs. They simply don't understand what makes a Cancerian tick – why do they worry themselves sick over things that they can't change? The Aquarian finds it all most peculiar. They also find it difficult to understand a Scorpio who takes so many things so seriously. Although the Aquarian also has a list of topics that mean a lot to them, they're not the sort of things that hold the slightest interest for a Scorpio. It's more or less the same story with a Pisces, because their huge resources of emotion make the Aquarian feel uncomfortable and fill them with a strong desire to escape as fast as possible.

Pisces

Relationships mean a lot to a sensitive Piscean, but they're easily misunderstood by many of the more robust signs. There are no such worries with the other Water signs, however. A Piscean loves being with a tender Cancerian who knows how to help them relax and feel safe. They really enjoy playing house together but the emotional scenes will blow the roof off. The relationship between a Piscean and a Scorpio can be quite spicy and sexy, but the Piscean is turned off if the Scorpio becomes too intense and dramatic. Two Pisceans feel safe with one another, but they'll push all their problems under the carpet unless one of them is more objective.

A Piscean also gets on well with the Earth signs, although with a few reservations. A Piscean takes comfort from being looked after by a protective Taurean, but after a while they could feel stifled by the Taurean's possessive and matter-of-fact attitude. The relationship between a Piscean and a Virgo starts off well but the Piscean could soon feel crushed by the Virgo's criticism and will need more emotional reassurance than the Virgo is able to give. A Piscean feels safe with a Capricorn because they're so dependable but in the end this may begin to bug them. It's not that they want the Capricorn to two-time them, more that they'd like a little unpredictability every now and then.

A Piscean is fascinated by the Air signs but their apparent lack of emotion could cause problems. A Piscean and a Gemini are terrific friends but could encounter difficulties as lovers. The Piscean's strong emotional needs are too much for the Gemini to handle – they'll feel as if they're drowning. The Piscean is on much firmer ground with a Libran, who'll go out of their way to keep the Piscean happy. Neither sign is good at facing up to any nasty truths, however. An Aquarian is too much for a sensitive Piscean, who views the world through rose-coloured specs. An Aquarian, on the other hand, has uncomfortably clear vision.

The Fire signs can cheer up a Piscean enormously, but any prolonged displays of emotion will make the Fire signs feel weighed down. The Piscean is fascinated by an Arien's exploits but could feel reluctant to join in. They'll also be easily hurt by some of the Arien's off-the-cuff remarks. When a Piscean pairs up with a Leo they appreciate the way the Leo wants to take charge and look after them. After a while, however, this could grate on them and they'll want to be more independent. A Piscean enjoys discussing philosophy and spiritual ideas with a Sagittarian – they can sit up half the night talking things through. The Sagittarian brand of honesty could hurt the Piscean at times, but they know this isn't malicious and will quickly forgive such outbursts.

Aries

Because Ariens belong to the Fire element, they get on very well with their fellow Fire signs Leo and Sagittarius. All the same, an Arien getting together with a Leo will soon notice a distinct drop in their bank balance, because they'll enjoy going to all the swankiest restaurants and sitting in the best seats at the theatre. When an Arien pairs up with a Sagittarian, they'll compete over who drives the fastest car and has the most exciting holidays. When two Ariens get together the results can be combustible. Ideally, one Arien should be a lot quieter, otherwise they'll spend most of their time jostling for power. All these combinations are very sexy and physical.

Ariens also thrive in the company of the three Air signs – Gemini, Libra and Aquarius. Of the three, they get on best with Geminis, who share their rather childlike view of the world and also their sense of fun. An Arien and a Gemini enjoy hatching all sorts of ideas and schemes, even if they never get round to putting them into action. There's an exciting sense of friction between Aries and Libra, their opposite number in the zodiac. An Arien will be enchanted by the way their Libran caters to their every need, but may become impatient when the Libran also wants to look after other people. An Arien will be captivated by the originality of an Aquarian, although at times they'll be driven mad by the Aquarian's eccentric approach to life and the way they blow hot and cold in the bedroom.

Ariens don't do so well with the Earth signs – Taurus, Virgo and Capricorn. The very careful, slightly plodding nature of a typical Taurean can drive an Arien barmy at times, and although they'll respect – and benefit from – the Taurean's practical approach to life, it can still fill them with irritation. An Arien finds it difficult to fathom a Virgo, because their attitudes to life are diametrically opposed. An Arien likes to jump in with both feet, while a Virgo prefers to take things slowly and analyse every possibility before committing themselves. An Arien can get on quite well with a Capricorn, because they're linked by their sense of ambition and their earthy sexual needs.

An Arien is out of their depth with any of the Water signs – Cancer, Scorpio and Pisces. They quickly become irritated by the defensive Cancerian, although they'll love their cooking. An Arien will enjoy a very passionate affair with a Scorpio, but the Scorpio's need to know exactly what the Arien is up to when their back is turned will soon cause problems and rifts. Although an Arien may begin a relationship with a Pisces by wanting to look after them and protect them from the harsh realities of life, eventually the Piscean's extremely sensitive nature may bring out the Arien's bullying streak.

Taurus

Taureans are literally in their element when they're with Virgos or Capricorns who, like themselves, are Earth signs. Two Taureans will get along very happily together, although they could become so wedded to routine that they get stuck in a rut. They may also encourage one another to eat too much. A Taurean will enjoy being with a Virgo, because they respect the Virgo's methodical nature. They'll also like encouraging their Virgo to relax and take life easy. Money will form a link between a Taurean and a Capricorn, with plenty of serious discussions on how to make it and what to do with it once they've got it. There will also be a strong sexual rapport, and the Taurean will encourage the more sensual side of the Capricorn.

The relationship between a Taurean and members of the Water element is also very good. A Taurean and a Cancerian will revel in one another's company and will probably be so happy at home that they'll rarely stir from their armchairs. They both have a strong need for emotional security and will stick together through thick and thin. There's plenty of passion when a Taurean pairs up with a Scorpio, although the faithful Taurean could become fed up with the Scorpio's jealous nature. They simply won't understand what they're being accused of, and their loyal nature will be offended by the very thought that they could be a two-timer. A Taurean will be delighted by a delicate Piscean, and will want to take care of such a vulnerable and sensitive creature.

Things become rather more complicated when a Taurean pairs up with an Arien, Leo or Sagittarian, all of whom are Fire signs. They have very little in common – Taureans like to take things slowly while Fire signs want to make things happen *now*. It's particularly difficult between a Taurean and an Arien – the careful Taurean will feel harried and rushed by the impetuous Arien. It's a little better when a Taurean gets together with a Leo, because they share a deep appreciation of the good things in life, although the Taurean will be horrified by the Leo's ability to spend money. Making joint decisions could be difficult, however, because they'll both stand their ground and refuse to budge. A Taurean and a Sagittarian simply don't understand each other – they're on such different wavelengths. Any Taurean displays of possessiveness will make the independent Sagittarian want to run a mile.

Taureans are equally mystified by the Air signs – Gemini, Libra and Aquarius. What they see as the flightiness of Gemini drives them barmy – why can't the Gemini settle down and do one thing at a time? The Taurean will probably feel quite exhausted by the Gemini's many interests and bubbly character. Taurus and Libra are a surprisingly good pairing, because they share a need for beauty, luxury and love. This could end up costing the penny-wise Taurean quite a packet, but they'll have a deliciously romantic time along the way. Taurus and Aquarius are chalk and cheese, and neither one is prepared to meet the other one halfway. The Taurean need to keep tabs on their loved one's every movement will irritate the freedom-loving Aquarian, and there will be plenty of rows as a result.

Gemini

One of the Air signs, Geminis get on very well with their fellow members of this element – Librans and Aquarians. Two Geminis are the astrological equivalent of double trouble – they chat nineteen to the dozen and revel in the company of someone who understands them so well. A Gemini delights in being with a Libran, because they enjoy the intellectual company and will benefit from the Libran's (usually) relaxed approach to life. They'll also learn to deal with their emotions more if a sympathetic Libran can guide them. Gemini and Aquarius is a very exciting pairing – the Gemini is encouraged to think deeply and knows that the Aquarian won't put up with any woolly ideas or fudged arguments.

Geminis also get on well with the three Fire signs – Aries, Leo and Sagittarius. A Gemini loves being with a racy, adventurous Arien, and together they enjoy keeping abreast of all the latest gossip and cultural developments. However, after the first flush of enthusiasm has worn off, the Gemini may find the Arien's strong need for sex rather hard to take. The Gemini gets on very well with a Leo. They delight in the Leo's affectionate nature and are amused by their need to have the best that money can buy – and they'll gladly share in the spoils. Gemini and Sagittarius are an excellent combination, because they sit opposite each other in the zodiac and so complement one another's character. The Gemini will be fascinated by the erudite and knowledgeable Sagittarian.

Gemini doesn't do so well with the Earth signs of Taurus and Capricorn, although they get on better with Virgo. The Gemini finds it difficult to understand a Taurean, because they see the world from such different viewpoints. The Gemini takes a more light-hearted approach and lives life at such a speed that they find it difficult to slow down to the more measured pace of a Taurean. The wonderfully dry Capricorn sense of humour is a source of constant delight to a Gemini. However, they're less taken with the Capricorn's streak of pessimism and their love of tradition. Of the three Earth signs, Gemini and Virgo are the most compatible. The Gemini shares the Virgo's brain power and they have long, fascinating conversations.

When a Gemini gets together with the Water signs, the result can be enjoyable or puzzling. Gemini and Cancer have little in common, because the Gemini wants to spread their emotional and intellectual wings, whereas a Cancerian likes to stay close to home and has little interest in abstract ideas. Gemini finds Scorpio perplexing because they operate on such different levels. A Gemini tends to skim along the surface of things, so often deals with life on a superficial level, whereas a Scorpio likes to dig deep and has to have an emotional investment in everything they do. A Gemini appreciates the subtlety and sensitivity of a Piscean, but they're likely to make off-the-cuff comments that unwittingly hurt the Piscean.

Cancer

Cancerians revel in the company of their fellow Water signs of Scorpio and Pisces. When two Cancerians get together they could spend most of their time at home or eating – preferably both. They feel safe in the knowledge that they both have a strong need for love, but their innate Cancerian tenacity may mean they cling on to the relationship even if it's long past its best. A Cancerian is enchanted with a Scorpio, because at last they feel free to really let rip emotionally. However, the intuitive Cancerian should beware of soaking up the Scorpio's darker moods like a psychic sponge. A Cancerian will take one look at a delicate Piscean and want to invite them home for a good hot meal. All the Cancerian's protective instincts are aroused by a gentle Piscean, but their anger will also be aroused if it turns out the Piscean has been leading a double life behind their back.

Cancerians also find a great deal of comfort in the company of the Earth signs – Taurus, Virgo and Capricorn. Cancer and Taurus were made for each other – they both adore home comforts and they trust one another implicitly. The Cancerian loves making a cosy nest for their hard-working Taurean. A Cancerian finds a Virgo a more difficult proposition, especially emotionally. Whereas Cancer is all warm hugs and holding hands by the fire, Virgo prefers to read a book and reserve any displays of affection for the bedroom. Cancer and Capricorn are opposite numbers in the zodiac, so share a tremendous rapport. They also share the same values of home, tradition and family, and if anyone can help a Capricorn to relax and take life easy, it's a Cancerian.

Life becomes more difficult when it comes to a Cancerian's relationship with any of the Air signs. They simply don't understand one another. A Cancerian can't make a Gemini out. They feel confused by what they think of as the Gemini's flightiness and inability to stay in one place for long. They can also be easily hurt by the Gemini's difficulty in expressing their emotions. A Cancerian gets on much better with a Libran. They're both ambitious in their own ways and so have a great deal in common. The Cancerian enjoys the Libran's romantic nature, but the Cancerian tendency to cling doesn't go down well. A Cancerian regards a typical Aquarian as a being from another planet. They're hurt by the Aquarian's strong need for independence and dislike of having to account for their every action, and are dismayed and confused by the Aquarian's hot-and-cold attitude to sex.

The Fire signs of Aries, Leo and Sagittarius are also a potential source of bewilderment to the gentle Cancerian. They understand the drive and ambition of an Arien, but will be stung by their blunt speech and worried about their daredevil tendencies. What if they hurt themselves? A Cancerian gets on well with a Leo because they share a strong love of family and are both openly affectionate and loving. The Cancerian enjoys creating a home that the Leo can feel proud of. So far, so good, but the story isn't so simple when a Cancerian pairs up with a Sagittarian. They're too different to understand one another – the Cancerian wants to stay at home with the family while the Sagittarian has an instinctive need to roam the world. As a result, the Cancerian will be disappointed, and then hurt, when the Sagittarian's busy schedule takes them away from home too often.

Leo

Leos adore the company of their fellow Fire signs, Aries and Sagittarius. They understand one another and enjoy each other's spontaneous warmth and affection. A Leo is amused by the exuberance and impulsiveness of an Arien, and they enjoy being persuaded to let their hair down a bit and not worry too much about appearances. A Leo enjoys the dash and vitality of a Sagittarian, although they may feel irritated if they can never get hold of them on the phone or the Sagittarian is always off doing other things. Two Leos together either love or loathe one another. One of them should be prepared to take a back seat, otherwise they'll both be vying for the limelight all the time.

The three Air signs of Gemini, Libra and Aquarius all get on well with Leos. When a Leo pairs up with a Gemini, you can expect lots of laughter and plenty of fascinating conversations. The demonstrative Leo is able to help the Gemini be more openly affectionate and loving. Leo and Libra is a great combination, and the Leo is enchanted by the Libran's fair-minded attitude. Both signs love luxury and all the good things in life but their bank managers may not be so pleased by the amount of money they manage to spend. Leo and Aquarius sit opposite one another across the horoscope, so they already have a great deal in common. They're fascinated by one another but they're both very stubborn, so any disputes between them usually end in stalemate because neither is prepared to concede any ground.

Leos don't really understand the Earth signs. Although Leos admire their practical approach to life, they find it rather restricting. A Leo enjoys the sensuous and hedonistic side of a Taurean's character but may become frustrated by their fear of change. Leo and Virgo have very little in common, especially when it comes to food – the Leo wants to tuck in at all the best restaurants while the Virgo is worried about the state of the kitchens, the number of calories and the size of the bill. A Leo respects the Capricorn's desire to support their family and approves of their need to be seen in the best possible light, but they feel hurt by the Capricorn's difficulty in showing their feelings.

When a Leo gets together with one of the Water signs – Cancer, Scorpio or Pisces – they'll enjoy the sexual side of the relationship but could eventually feel stifled by all that Watery emotion. A Leo and a Cancerian adore making a home together and both dote on their children. The Leo also likes comforting their vulnerable Cancerian – provided this doesn't happen too often. A Leo and a Scorpio will be powerfully attracted to one another, but power could also pull them apart – who's going to wear the trousers? They'll also lock horns during rows and both of them will refuse to back down. A Leo delights in a sophisticated Piscean, but may become irritated by their indecision and jangly nerves.

Virgo

As you might imagine, Virgos are happy with their fellow Earth signs of Taurus and Capricorn because they share the same practical attitude. A Virgo enjoys the steady, reassuring company of a Taurean, and they might even learn to relax a little instead of worrying themselves into the ground over the slightest problem. When two Virgos get together it can be too much of a good thing. Although at first they'll love talking to someone who shares so many of their preoccupations and ideas, they can soon drive one another round the bend. When a Virgo first meets a Capricorn they're delighted to know someone who's obviously got their head screwed on. It's only later on that they wish the Capricorn could lighten up every now and then.

Virgos get on well with Cancerians, Scorpios and Pisceans, the three Water signs. A Virgo enjoys being looked after by a considerate Cancerian, although they'll worry about their waistline and may get irritated by the Cancerian's super-sensitive feelings. You can expect plenty of long, analytical conversations when a Virgo gets together with a Scorpio. They both love getting to the bottom of subjects and will endlessly talk things through. They'll also get on extremely well in the bedroom. Pisces is Virgo's opposite sign, but although some opposites thrive in each other's company, that isn't always the case with this combination. The Virgo could soon grow impatient with the dreamy Piscean and will long to tell them a few home truths.

Although the other Earth signs don't usually get on well with Air signs, it's different for Virgos. They understand the intellectual energies of Geminis, Librans and Aquarians. A Virgo thrives in a Gemini's company, and they spend hours chatting over the phone if they can't get together in person. It's difficult for them to discuss their emotions, however, and they may never tell each other how they really feel. A Virgo admires a sophisticated, charming Libran, and marvels at their diplomacy. How do they do it? Expect a few sparks to fly when a Virgo pairs up with an Aquarian, because both of them have very strong opinions and aren't afraid to air them. The result is a lot of hot air and some vigorous arguments.

The three Fire signs – Aries, Leo and Sagittarius – are a source of endless fascination to a Virgo. They've got so much energy! A Virgo finds an Arien exciting but their relationship could be short-lived because the Virgo will be so irritated by the Arien's devil-may-care attitude to life. When a Virgo pairs up with a Leo, they'll be intrigued by this person's comparatively lavish lifestyle but their own modest temperament will be shocked if the Leo enjoys showing off. A Virgo is able to talk to a Sagittarius until the cows come home – they're both fascinated by ideas, although the precise Virgo will first be amused, and then irritated, by the Sagittarian's rather relaxed attitude to hard facts.

Libra

Of all the members of the zodiac, this is the one that finds it easiest to get on with the other signs. Librans get on particularly well with Geminis and Aquarians, their fellow Air signs. A Libran is enchanted by a Gemini's quick brain and ready wit, and they enjoy endless discussions on all sorts of subjects. When two Librans get together, they revel in the resulting harmonious atmosphere but it's almost impossible for them to reach any decisions – each one defers to the other while being unable to say what they really want. A Libran is intrigued by the independence and sharp mind of an Aquarian, but their feelings could be hurt by the Aquarian's emotional coolness.

Libra enjoys being with the three Fire signs – Aries, Leo and Sagittarius. Libra, who often takes life at rather a slow pace, is energized by a lively Arien, and they complement one another's personalities well. However, the Libran may occasionally feel hurt by the Arien's single-mindedness and blunt speech. A Libran adores the luxury-loving ways of a Leo, and they'll both spend a fortune in the pursuit of happiness. They also get on well in the bedroom. When a Libran gets together with an exuberant Sagittarian, they'll have great fun. All the same, the Sagittarian need for honesty could fluster the Libran, who adopts a much more diplomatic approach to life.

Although the other two Air signs can find it hard to understand members of the Water element, it's different for Librans. They're more sympathetic to the emotional energies of Cancerians, Scorpios and Pisceans. A Libran delights in the protective care of a Cancerian, but those ever-changing Cancerian moods may be hard for a balanced Libran to take. Those deep Scorpio emotions will intrigue the Libran but they may quickly become bogged down by such an intense outlook on life and will be desperate for some light relief. As for Pisces, the Libran is charmed by the Piscean's delicate nature and creative gifts, but both signs hate facing up to unpleasant facts so this couple may never deal with any problems that lie between them.

Libra enjoys the reliable natures of Taurus, Virgo and Capricorn, the Earth signs. A Libran appreciates the company of a relaxed and easy-going Taurean, although they may sometimes regret the Taurean's lack of imagination. When a Libran and a Virgo get together, the Libran enjoys the Virgo's mental abilities but their critical comments will soon cut the Libran to the quick. The Libran may not come back for a second tongue-lashing. A Libran understands the ambitions of a Capricorn, and likes their steady nature and the way they support their family. However, there could soon be rows about money, with the Libran spending a lot more than the Capricorn thinks is necessary.

Compatibility in Love and Sex at a glance

M \ F	♈	♉	♊	♋	♌	♍	♎	♏	♐	♑	♒	♓
♈	8	5	9	7	9	4	7	8	9	7	7	3
♉	6	8	4	10	7	8	8	7	3	8	2	8
♊	8	2	7	3	8	7	9	4	9	4	9	4
♋	5	10	4	8	6	5	6	8	2	9	2	8
♌	9	8	9	7	7	4	9	6	8	7	9	6
♍	4	8	6	4	4	7	6	7	7	9	4	4
♎	7	8	10	7	8	5	9	6	9	6	10	6
♏	7	9	4	7	6	6	7	10	5	6	5	7
♐	9	4	10	4	9	7	8	4	9	6	9	5
♑	7	8	4	9	6	8	6	4	4	8	4	5
♒	8	6	9	4	9	4	9	6	8	7	8	2
♓	7	6	7	9	6	7	6	9	7	5	4	9

1 = the pits
10 = the peaks

Key

♈ - Aries
♉ - Taurus
♊ - Gemini
♋ - Cancer
♌ - Leo
♍ - Virgo
♎ - Libra
♏ - Scorpio
♐ - Sagittarius
♑ - Capricorn
♒ - Aquarius
♓ - Pisces

Compatibility in Friendship at a glance

M \ F	♈	♉	♊	♋	♌	♍	♎	♏	♐	♑	♒	♓
♈	8	5	10	5	9	3	7	8	9	6	8	5
♉	6	9	6	10	7	8	7	6	4	9	3	9
♊	9	3	9	4	9	8	10	5	10	5	10	6
♋	6	9	4	9	5	4	6	9	4	10	3	9
♌	10	7	9	6	9	4	8	6	9	6	9	7
♍	5	9	8	4	4	8	5	8	8	10	5	6
♎	8	9	10	8	8	6	9	5	9	6	10	7
♏	7	8	5	8	7	7	6	9	4	5	6	8
♐	9	5	10	4	10	8	8	4	10	7	9	6
♑	6	9	5	10	6	9	5	5	4	9	5	6
♒	9	6	10	5	9	5	9	7	9	5	9	3
♓	6	7	6	10	6	8	7	9	8	6	4	10

1 = the pits
10 = the peaks

Key

♈ - Aries
♉ - Taurus
♊ - Gemini
♋ - Cancer
♌ - Leo
♍ - Virgo
♎ - Libra
♏ - Scorpio
♐ - Sagittarius
♑ - Capricorn
♒ - Aquarius
♓ - Pisces

YOUR POTENTIAL AND CREATIVITY

Have you ever wondered if you're living up to your Sun sign's potential? Have you been curious to know if you have other skills that you've yet to explore? Do you feel as though something is missing from your life? If you've answered 'yes' to any of these questions, read on to discover how to make the best of your Sun sign.

Scorpio

You store so many of your experiences deep inside you that it's important to find constructive and creative outlets for them. Writing down your thoughts in a diary is one option, or maybe you'd prefer to do something rather more dramatic, such as performing poetry? As a Scorpio you are naturally attuned to the areas in life that many of us shy away from, so you could gain tremendous fulfilment from becoming a bereavement counsellor, working with people who have Aids or being a volunteer in a hospice. You would have the satisfaction of knowing you were doing something truly valuable. On a lighter note, many Scorpios are wine buffs, so how about going on a wine tasting course or teaching yourself to appreciate wine? Think of the fun you'd have!

Sagittarius

You have such an open mind that you're always interested in finding new ways to express yourself. You've probably already worked your way through a string of different interests and you know there are plenty more where those came from. If you're stuck for ideas, how about developing something that's already a theme in your life? If you enjoy travel, you might decide to learn a foreign language. It will give you a big kick to go abroad and chat away to the locals in their own tongue. If you're interested in history, you might decide to study a particular period in great detail, or collect items that date from that period. Activities that improve the environment may also appeal to you, and you might even end up getting involved in politics!

Capricorn

Have you ever thought of rock climbing? After all, you do belong to the sign of the mountain goat! Even if you can't bear the thought of dangling off a cliff face, you might like the idea of doing some hill walking or rambling. They'd be good antidotes to all those hours you spend at work. Alternatively, if you're looking for an unusual pet, how about keeping a goat? Any activities that help you to express your reliability are good for you, although you must make sure you aren't saddled with all the tasks that no one else wants to do. You might consider learning accountancy so that you can sort out your own finances and those of your friends, or learning the intricacies of the stock market so you can start making some clever investments.

Aquarius

If you're currently wondering how to give your life more meaning, have you considered doing something that brings out your humanitarian streak? You have a very rational view of the world that deserves a wider audience. You might get involved in a charity by giving regular donations, or you could decide to lend a hand in other ways, such as volunteering your time. Alternatively, you could be interested in politics, especially if you get fed up shouting at the television when you hear about things you don't agree with. You could soon be shouting at fellow councillors or MPs! If you're fascinated by outer space, how about buying yourself a telescope and a star map? You'll also love learning about the science of astronomy. Watching a science fiction film will never be the same again!

Pisces

If you're looking for new ways to express your Piscean talents, swimming is something that might appeal. Surprisingly, given that this is the sign of the fish, many Pisceans aren't very good at swimming, so you could combine swimming lessons with regular exercise. Dance is another Piscean activity, whether you're doing the dancing or watching someone else. It's certainly very important for you to do something that allows you to express yourself, otherwise you'll feel stifled and unfulfilled. You might be interested in learning aromatherapy or working with crystals, and your powerful intuition could make you a natural tarot reader or caster of the runes. You'll also enjoy the slightly mysterious aspects of it all.

Aries

Two of your greatest strengths are your fiery enthusiasm and your enjoyment in being a daredevil. You don't want to stand on the sidelines when you could be right in the thick of things. Even if you aren't really risking life and limb, you like to imagine that you are. Any activity that brings excitement into your life and appeals to your intrepid spirit will suit you well. How about rock climbing, hang-gliding or bungee jumping? They'll all get the adrenalin flowing! You're also ace at sports and athletics, so you might decide to show off your skills on the football or rugby pitch. Being an explorer also appeals to you, so you'll get a real buzz from being the first in your social circle to do something new. With luck, you'll start a trend!

Taurus

Any activity that draws on your resolute character and your practical nature will bring out the best in you. You're also extremely artistic so will enjoy expressing your creative talents. Anything that brings you into contact with the great outdoors is perfect for you. For instance, gardening might be an ideal occupation for you. You thoroughly enjoy working with nature, and being out in the fresh air helps you to clear your head and get problems in perspective. Taurus is the sign that rules beautiful voices, so how about taking singing lessons? Even if you think you can't sing a note, you'll really enjoy discovering your natural voice and using it as a vehicle for self-expression. If you have a sweet tooth, you may also enjoy making your own chocolates. But don't be surprised if you're deluged with requests from friends!

Gemini

Anything that allows you to communicate is right up your street. If you've always toyed with the idea of writing a novel or becoming a journalist but have never done anything about it, it isn't too late to start! Even keeping a regular journal will encourage you to put your thoughts down on paper and you'll soon find it becomes second nature. Who knows where it might lead! Geminis are noted for their ability to think quickly and analytically, so you might enjoy teaching yourself how to do logic puzzles or cryptic crosswords. Or maybe you'd enjoy showing off your range of knowledge in a pub quiz? This is the sign that rules the hands, so if you're looking for a sideline you might consider training to be a manicurist – or maybe you'd like to teach yourself palmistry!

Cancer

You belong to the sign of the homemaker, so anything that will improve the atmosphere or appearance of your home is a natural choice for you. You might decide to learn how to make soft furnishings, you could stitch a needlepoint cushion or even a rug if you're feeling ambitious, or you could train to be an interior decorator. Cancerians are often fascinated by the past, so you might decide to research your family tree or organize all the family photographs into chronological order. If you want to take this one step further, how about signing up for a history course or taking a class in antiques? Cooking is another wonderful way for you to express yourself, and if you're good at it you can expect lots of encouragement from your family and friends!

Leo

You have a head start because you belong to one of the most creative signs of all. If you've always fancied treading the boards but have never fancied it as a career, you might consider joining an amateur dramatics group. It might satisfy your instinctive Leo yearning to be in the limelight. Alternatively, how about joining a poetry circle or writing group in which you can perform your work? Many Leos are born artists, so you might be interested in learning how to paint or draw. Or perhaps you'd like to do something slightly different, such as painting silk scarves or making stained-glass windows or jewellery? You can also find it inspiring to put your terrific organizational skills to good use.

Virgo

You have a marvellous eye for detail, good manual dexterity and astonishing reserves of patience, so you might enjoy doing something that draws on these talents. You could develop a passion for jigsaws, for instance! If you want to do something practical, perhaps even that you can sell to make some money, how about teaching yourself a very fiddly skill such as lace-making, découpage, mosaics or embroidery? With your interest in health matters and your Virgoan need to serve others, you might consider taking up medicine professionally. If you feel it's too late to train to be a doctor or nurse, how about learning chiropody or one of the complementary therapies? If you prefer to do something with figures, you could consider taking a course in higher mathematics or accountancy. Very useful!

Libra

You belong to one of the two most attractive signs of all, so you might enjoy making the most of it! For instance, you could decide to learn a beauty therapy or anything else that makes people feel good. Training to be an aromatherapist or masseur could appeal to you. You enjoy the sensual feel of natural fabrics such as velvet and silk, so how about doing some dressmaking? You might become so good at it that you end up making clothes for other people as well – and being paid for it! Don't overlook your diplomatic skills either. If you were considering doing some voluntary work, for instance, you might be excellent working on a phoneline or doing some sort of counselling. You would easily be able to combine compassion with objectivity.

BORN ON THE CUSP?

Were you born on the cusp of Scorpio – at the beginning or end of the sign? If so, you may have spent years wondering which sign you belong to. Are you a Scorpio, a Libran or a Sagittarian? Different horoscope books and columns can give different dates for when the Sun moves into each sign, leaving you utterly confused. Yet none of these dates is wrong, as you'll discover in a minute. Checking your birth date, and time if you know it, in the list given in this chapter will allow you to solve the mystery at long last!

Many people believe that the Sun moves like clockwork from one sign to another on a specific day each year. But this isn't always true. For instance, let's look at the dates for the sign of Scorpio. On the cover of this book I give them as 24 October to 22 November. Very often, the Sun will obediently change signs on these days but sometimes it won't. It can move from Libra into Scorpio on 22, 23 or 24 October and it can move from Scorpio into Sagittarius on 22 or 23 November.

So how can you find out which sign you belong to if you were born on the cusp of Scorpio? The only information you need is the place, year, day and the time of your birth if you know it. It helps to have the time of birth because if the Sun did move signs on your birthday, you can see whether it moved before or after you were born. If you don't have an exact time, even knowing whether it was morning or afternoon can be a help. For instance, if you were born in the morning and the Sun didn't move signs on your birthday until the afternoon, that will be enough information to tell you which sign is yours.

You need to know the place in case you were born outside the United Kingdom and have to convert its local time zone to British time. This information is easily available in many diaries and reference books.

Four Simple Steps to Find your Sun Sign

1 Write down the year, day, time and place of your birth, in that order.

2 If you were born outside the United Kingdom, you must convert your birth date and time to British time by adding or subtracting the relevant number of hours from your birth time to convert it to British time. This may take your birthday into the following day or back to the previous day. If so, write down this new date and time because that will be the one you use in the following calculations. If summer time was operating you must deduct the relevant number of hours to convert your birth time to Greenwich Mean Time (GMT).

3 If you were born in Britain, look up your year of birth in the list of British Summer Time (BST) changes to see if BST was operating when you were born. If it was, subtract the appropriate number of hours from your birth time to convert it to GMT. This may give you a different time and/or date of birth.

4 Look up your year of birth in the Annual Sun Sign Changes list. If you were born within these dates and times, you are a Scorpio. If you were born outside them, you are either a Libran if you were born in October, or a Sagittarian if you were born in November.

Two Examples

Here are a couple of examples so you can see how the process works. Let's say we're looking for the Sun sign of Paul, who was born in the UK on 24 October 1965 at 00:30. Start by checking the list of British Summer Time dates to see if BST was operating at the time of his birth. It was, so you have to subtract one hour from his birth time to convert it to GMT. This gives him a birth time of 23:30 on the previous day – therefore, his GMT birthday is 23 October and his GMT birth time is 23:30. Write this down, so you don't forget it. Now turn to the Annual Sun Sign Changes list and look for 1965, his year of birth. In that year, the Sun moved into Scorpio on 23 October at 15:11, and Paul's GMT birth time was at 23:30 that day, so he is a Scorpio. However, if he had been born on 23 October 1963 (note the change of year) at 23:30 (which gives him a GMT birth time of 22:30), the Sun would have been in Libra so he would be a Libran.

But what would his sign be if he were born on 22 November 1965 at 12:30? First, check the dates in the BST list for 1965 to see if it was operating at the time of his birth. It wasn't, so his birth time and day remain the same. Now look up the Sun sign dates for 1965. Look at the November date. The Sun was in Scorpio until 22 November at 12:29. So Paul was born just after the Sun had moved into Sagittarius, making him a Sagittarian.

Dates for British Summer Time

If your birthday falls within these dates and times, you were born during BST and will have to convert your birth time back to GMT. To do this, subtract one hour from your birth time. If you were born during a period that is marked *, you must subtract two hours from your birth time to convert it to GMT. All times are given in BST, using the 24-hour clock.

1920 28 Mar, 02:00–25 Oct, 01:59 inc
1921 3 Apr, 02:00–3 Oct, 01:59 inc
1922 26 Mar, 02:00–8 Oct, 01:59 inc
1923 22 Apr, 02:00–16 Sep, 01:59 inc
1924 13 Apr, 02:00–21 Sep, 01:59 inc
1925 19 Apr, 02:00–4 Oct, 01:59 inc
1926 18 Apr, 02:00–3 Oct, 01:59 inc
1927 10 Apr, 02:00–2 Oct, 01:59 inc
1928 22 Apr, 02:00–7 Oct, 01:59 inc
1929 21 Apr, 02:00–6 Oct, 01:59 inc
1930 13 Apr, 02:00–5 Oct, 01:59 inc
1931 19 Apr, 02:00–4 Oct, 01:59 inc
1932 17 Apr, 02:00–2 Oct, 01:59 inc
1933 9 Apr, 02:00–8 Oct, 01:59 inc
1934 22 Apr, 02:00–7 Oct, 01:59 inc
1935 14 Apr, 02:00–6 Oct, 01:59 inc
1936 19 Apr, 02:00–4 Oct, 01:59 inc
1937 18 Apr, 02:00–3 Oct, 01:59 inc
1938 10 Apr, 02:00–2 Oct, 01:59 inc
1939 16 Apr, 02:00–19 Nov, 01:59 inc
1940 25 Feb, 02:00–31 Dec, 23:59 inc
1941 1 Jan, 00:00–4 May, 01:59 inc
1941 4 May, 02:00–10 Aug, 01:59 inc*
1941 10 Aug, 02:00–31 Dec, 23:59 inc
1942 1 Jan, 00:00–5 Apr, 01:59 inc
1942 5 Apr, 02:00–9 Aug, 01:59 inc*
1942 9 Aug, 02:00–31 Dec, 23:59 inc
1943 1 Jan, 00:00–4 Apr, 01:59 inc
1943 4 Apr, 02:00–15 Aug, 01:59 inc*
1943 15 Aug, 02:00–31 Dec, 23:59 inc
1944 1 Jan, 00:00–2 Apr, 01:59 inc
1944 2 Apr, 02:00–17 Sep, 01:59 inc*
1944 17 Sep, 02:00–31 Dec, 23:59 inc
1945 1 Jan, 02:00–2 Apr, 01:59 inc
1945 2 Apr, 02:00–15 Jul, 01:59 inc*
1945 15 Jul, 02:00–7 Oct, 01:59 inc
1946 14 Apr, 02:00–6 Oct, 01:59 inc
1947 16 Mar, 02:00–13 Apr, 01:59 inc
1947 13 Apr, 02:00–10 Aug, 01:59 inc*
1947 10 Aug, 02:00–2 Nov, 01:59 inc
1948 14 Mar, 02:00–31 Oct, 01:59 inc
1949 3 Apr, 02:00–30 Oct, 01:59 inc
1950 16 Apr, 02:00–22 Oct, 01:59 inc
1951 15 Apr, 02:00–21 Oct, 01:59 inc
1952 20 Apr, 02:00–26 Oct, 01:59 inc
1953 19 Apr, 02:00–4 Oct, 01:59 inc
1954 11 Apr, 02:00–3 Oct, 01:59 inc
1955 17 Apr, 02:00–2 Oct, 01:59 inc
1956 22 Apr, 02:00–7 Oct, 01:59 inc
1957 14 Apr, 02:00–6 Oct, 01:59 inc
1958 20 Apr, 02:00–5 Oct, 01:59 inc
1959 19 Apr, 02:00–4 Oct, 01:59 inc
1960 10 Apr, 02:00–2 Oct, 01:59 inc
1961 26 Mar, 02:00–29 Oct, 01:59 inc
1962 25 Mar, 02:00–28 Oct, 01:59 inc
1963 31 Mar, 02:00–27 Oct, 01:59 inc
1964 22 Mar, 02:00–25 Oct, 01:59 inc
1965 21 Mar, 02:00–24 Oct, 01:59 inc
1966 20 Mar, 02:00–23 Oct, 01:59 inc
1967 19 Mar, 02:00–29 Oct, 01:59 inc
1968 18 Feb, 02:00–31 Dec, 23:59 inc
1969 1 Jan, 00:00–31 Dec, 23:59 inc
1970 1 Jan, 00:00–31 Dec, 23:59 inc
1971 1 Jan, 00:00–31 Oct, 01:59 inc
1972 19 Mar, 02:00–29 Oct, 01:59 inc
1973 18 Mar, 02:00–28 Oct, 01:59 inc
1974 17 Mar, 02:00–27 Oct, 01:59 inc
1975 16 Mar, 02:00–26 Oct, 01:59 inc
1976 21 Mar, 02:00–24 Oct, 01:59 inc
1977 20 Mar, 02:00–23 Oct, 01:59 inc
1978 19 Mar, 02:00–29 Oct, 01:59 inc
1979 18 Mar, 02:00–28 Oct, 01:59 inc
1980 16 Mar, 02:00–26 Oct, 01:59 inc
1981 29 Mar, 01:00–25 Oct, 00:59 inc
1982 28 Mar, 01:00–24 Oct, 00:59 inc
1983 27 Mar, 01:00–23 Oct, 00:59 inc
1984 25 Mar, 01:00–28 Oct, 00:59 inc
1985 31 Mar, 01:00–27 Oct, 00:59 inc
1986 30 Mar, 01:00–26 Oct, 00:59 inc
1987 29 Mar, 01:00–25 Oct, 00:59 inc
1988 27 Mar, 01:00–23 Oct, 00:59 inc
1989 26 Mar, 01:00–29 Oct, 00:59 inc
1990 25 Mar, 01:00–28 Oct, 00:59 inc
1991 31 Mar, 01:00–27 Oct, 00:59 inc
1992 29 Mar, 01:00–25 Oct, 00:59 inc
1993 28 Mar, 01:00–24 Oct, 00:59 inc
1994 27 Mar, 01:00–23 Oct, 00:59 inc
1995 26 Mar, 01:00–22 Oct, 00:59 inc

1996 31 Mar, 01:00–27 Oct, 00:59 inc
1997 30 Mar, 01:00–26 Oct, 00:59 inc
1998 29 Mar, 01:00–25 Oct, 00:59 inc
1999 28 Mar, 01:00–31 Oct, 00:59 inc
2000 26 Mar, 01:00–29 Oct, 00:59 inc
2001 25 Mar, 01:00–28 Oct, 00:59 inc
2002 24 Mar, 01:00–27 Oct, 00:59 inc

* Subtract two hours from the birth time to convert it to GMT.

Annual Sun Sign Changes

If your birthday falls within these dates and times, you are a Scorpio. If you were born in October before the first date and time, you are a Libran. If you were born in November after the second date and time, you are a Sagittarian. All times are given in GMT, using the 24-hour clock.

1920 23 Oct, 17:13–22 Nov, 14:15 inc
1921 23 Oct, 23:03–22 Nov, 20:04 inc
1922 24 Oct, 04:53–23 Nov, 01:55 inc
1923 24 Oct, 10:51–23 Nov, 07:53 inc
1924 23 Oct, 16:45–22 Nov, 13:46 inc
1925 23 Oct, 22:32–22 Nov, 19:35 inc
1926 24 Oct, 04:19–23 Nov, 01:27 inc
1927 24 Oct, 10:07–23 Nov, 07:13 inc
1928 23 Oct, 15:55–22 Nov, 13:00 inc
1929 23 Oct, 21:42–22 Nov, 18:48 inc
1930 24 Oct, 03:26–23 Nov, 00:34 inc
1931 24 Oct, 09:16–23 Nov, 06:24 inc
1932 23 Oct, 15:04–22 Nov, 12:10 inc
1933 23 Oct, 20:49–22 Nov, 17:53 inc
1934 24 Oct, 02:37–22 Nov, 23.44 inc
1935 24 Oct, 08:30–23 Nov, 05:35 inc
1936 23 Oct, 14:19–22 Nov, 11:24 inc
1937 23 Oct, 20:07–22 Nov, 17:16 inc
1938 24 Oct, 01:54–22 Nov, 23:06 inc
1939 24 Oct, 07:46–23 Nov, 04:58 inc
1940 23 Oct, 13:40–22 Nov, 10:48 inc
1941 23 Oct, 19:28–22 Nov, 16:37 inc
1942 24 Oct, 01:16–22 Nov, 22:30 inc
1943 24 Oct, 07:09–23 Nov, 04:21 inc
1944 23 Oct, 12:56–22 Nov, 10:07 inc
1945 23 Oct, 18:44–22 Nov, 15:55 inc
1946 24 Oct, 00:35–22 Nov, 21:46 inc
1947 24 Oct, 06:26–23 Nov, 03:37 inc
1948 23 Oct, 12:18–22 Nov, 09:28 inc
1949 23 Oct, 18:03–22 Nov, 15:16 inc
1950 23 Oct, 23:45–22 Nov, 21:02 inc
1951 24 Oct, 05:37–23 Nov, 02:51 inc
1952 23 Oct, 11:23–22 Nov, 08:35 inc
1953 23 Oct, 17:07–22 Nov, 14:22 inc
1954 23 Oct, 22:57–22 Nov, 20:14 inc
1955 24 Oct, 04:44–23 Nov, 02:00 inc
1956 23 Oct, 10:35–22 Nov, 07:49 inc
1957 23 Oct, 16:25–22 Nov, 13:39 inc
1958 23 Oct, 22:12–22 Nov, 19:29 inc
1959 24 Oct, 04:12–23 Nov, 01:27 inc
1960 23 Oct, 10:02–22 Nov, 07:18 inc
1961 23 Oct, 15:48–22 Nov, 13:07 inc
1962 23 Oct, 21:41–22 Nov, 19:01 inc
1963 24 Oct, 03:29–23 Nov, 00:49 inc
1964 23 Oct, 09:21–22 Nov, 06:38 inc
1965 23 Oct, 15:11–22 Nov, 12:29 inc
1966 23 Oct, 20:51–22 Nov, 18:14 inc
1967 24 Oct, 02:44–23 Nov, 00:04 inc
1968 23 Oct, 08:30–22 Nov, 05:48 inc
1969 23 Oct, 14:12–22 Nov, 11:31 inc
1970 23 Oct, 20:05–22 Nov, 17:24 inc
1971 24 Oct, 01:54–22 Nov, 23:14 inc
1972 23 Oct, 07:42–22 Nov, 05:02 inc
1973 23 Oct, 13:31–22 Nov, 10:54 inc
1974 23 Oct, 19:11–22 Nov, 16:38 inc
1975 24 Oct, 01:07–22 Nov, 22:30 inc

1976 23 Oct, 06:59–22 Nov, 04:21 inc
1978 23 Oct, 18:38–22 Nov, 16:04 inc
1980 23 Oct, 06:18–22 Nov, 03:41 inc
1982 23 Oct, 17:59–22 Nov, 15:23 inc
1984 23 Oct, 05:47–22 Nov, 03:11 inc
1986 23 Oct, 17:15–22 Nov, 14:44 inc
1988 23 Oct, 04:45–22 Nov, 02:12 inc
1990 23 Oct, 16:15–22 Nov, 13:47 inc
1992 23 Oct, 03:58–22 Nov, 01:26 inc
1994 23 Oct, 15:37–22 Nov, 13:06 inc
1996 23 Oct, 03:20–22 Nov, 00:49 inc
1998 23 Oct, 15:00–22 Nov, 12:34 inc
2000 23 Oct, 02:49–22 Nov, 00:19 inc
2002 23 Oct, 14:19–22 Nov, 11:54 inc
1977 23 Oct, 12:41–22 Nov, 10:07 inc
1979 24 Oct, 00:29–22 Nov, 21:54 inc
1981 23 Oct, 12:14–22 Nov, 09:36 inc
1983 23 Oct, 23:55–22 Nov, 21:18 inc
1985 23 Oct, 11:23–22 Nov, 08:51 inc
1987 23 Oct, 23:02–22 Nov, 20:29 inc
1989 23 Oct, 10:36–22 Nov, 08:05 inc
1991 23 Oct, 22:06–22 Nov, 19:36 inc
1993 23 Oct, 09:38–22 Nov, 07:07 inc
1995 23 Oct, 21:33–22 Nov, 19:01 inc
1997 23 Oct, 09:16–22 Nov, 06:48 inc
1999 23 Oct, 20:53–22 Nov, 18:25 inc
2001 23 Oct, 08:27–22 Nov, 06:01 inc